WORDSWORTH:

LECTURES AND ESSAYS

BY

H. W. GARROD

Fellow of Merton College
Professor of Poetry in the
University of Oxford

Second Edition
Enlarged

OXFORD

AT THE CLARENDON PRESS

Oxford University Press, Amen House, London E.C.4

GLASGOW NEW YORK TORONTO MELBOURNE WELLINGTON
BOMBAY CALCUTTA MADRAS KARACHI LAHORE DACCA
CAPE TOWN SALISBURY NAIROBI IBADAN ACCRA
KUALA LUMPUR HONG KONG

FIRST EDITION 1923
SECOND EDITION 1927
REPRINTED 1939, 1949, 1954, 1958, 1963

PRINTED IN GREAT BRITAIN

PREFACE
TO THE SECOND EDITION

IN preparing a second edition of this book, I have corrected one or two errors of detail, and I have taken the opportunity of adding a new essay (*Dorothy Wordsworth*). The chapter upon the *Composition of The Prelude* I have left as it was. I could only bring it up to date by re-writing it; and it seemed simpler and more honest to refer the reader to Mr. de Sélincourt's edition of *The Prelude*. So far as I know, wherever Mr. de Sélincourt corrects me, I accept his corrections; and in saying this I should wish it to apply to other parts of my book, as well as to the chapter I mention. What I have said about *The Borderers* needs to be corrected in the light of Mr. de Sélincourt's article in the *Nineteenth Century*, Nov. 1926.

I had intended to alter the paragraph on pp. 16–17 which speaks of Bishop Christopher Wordsworth; not because it gave pain where I should be sorry to give it, but because I have reason to think it not true. I have preferred, however, not to change it, but to correct it by better authority than was then available to me. The paragraph brought me a letter from the late Mr. A. C. Benson; from which I am allowed to quote the following sentences:

> I have known many of the Wordsworth family intimately, and I cannot help wishing that you would revise your view of Bishop Christopher Wordsworth a little. I don't defend his

Preface to Second Edition

book—I think it a wretched performance; but he wasn't in the least a cautious conventional ecclesiastic. He was, of course, not a Bishop till many years after he wrote the book. He held very advanced views on many points—female education, for instance—and he was a man of almost Quixotic courage. He always seemed to be living in the third century A. D. . . . I can never understand how he came to write so *lifeless* a book . . . but, of course, he didn't understand him, though he had a good deal of poetical fervour himself . . . I won't labour the point. Anyone who knew Christopher Wordsworth, the Bishop, would not recognize him as you describe him—he was orthodox, in a way, but I don't expect that his thoughts ever dwelt very much on respectability.

I accept what is there said; and am sorry to have spoken ungenerously of a man of generous and courageous character. I was not the first offender; but I ought now to be the last.

H. W. G.

FROM THE PREFACE TO THE FIRST EDITION

NOT modesty, but common decency, obliges me to say that this book was provoked by two much better ones. Whether this gives it an excuse, or deprives it of one, I am not sure. The book is an amplification of a course of lectures delivered in Oxford, at the invitation of the Professor of English Literature, so long ago as the summer of 1919. When the lectures were first prepared, Mr. Harper's *William Wordsworth* still ranked as a new book. When I began to shape them for publication, M. Émile Legouis had just produced a second edition of his *Jeunesse de William Wordsworth*. What I owe to the stimulus of these two books (of which, however, I know the second only in its first edition) will be obvious, and is, I hope, sufficiently acknowledged in the text. I trust at the same time that I have reacted upon the stimulus with what I may call a manly, but not unmannerly, self-assertion. What my debt is to other books, I should find it difficult to say—some of them, that I might not be too much tied to better talents than my own, I have deliberately forborne to re-read. But I am moved to put on record here the ineffaceable impression left upon my mind by the period, now some thirty years since, when I first made acquaintance with Matthew Arnold's *Poems of Wordsworth*. As a critic of poetry Matthew Arnold is now thought, I am told, somewhat *démodé*. I think it a pity, for even if he marred by some degree of affectation

Preface to First Edition

and absurdity a good deal of his work, yet in general he brought to the study of poetry a sure and fine sense of the best; and his Wordsworth volume is a slender, but noble, monument of his supreme critical judgement.

I am conscious that my book carries with it some defects both of method and style which are incidental to the environment of the lecture-room. These, so far as was in my power, I have tried to remedy. But the days of liberal leisure are gone from us; and the book, I know, is at many points defective in arrangement, in some of its parts over-ample, and in others patently lacunous. Perhaps this is only another way of saying (what may not be true) that the books of all of us would be better if life were longer. The defects, however, of which I speak are of a kind the least easy to revise away; and they may, I hope, meet with charity, at least from those who know the difficulty of this kind of revision.

To the lectures of 1919 (sections I–X) I have added two essays which belong to the present year. Of these the first (XI) directly supplements the lectures. The second (XII) will interest only a special class of reader; for whose sake it is placed here. The general reader can leave it alone, and, like the allegory of the *Faerie Queene*, it will at least ' not bite him '.

Mr. D. Nichol Smith, Goldsmiths' Reader in English Literature, was kind enough to read the whole book in manuscript; and to his wide knowledge of the literature of Wordsworth, and his notoriously impeccable judgement, I am everywhere indebted. I have also to thank Professor D. A. Slater, of Liverpool, and Mr. R. W. Chapman, for much helpful criticism.

H. W. G.

November 1922.

CONTENTS

i. Biography and Autobiography *Page* 9

ii. *Descriptive Sketches* . . *Page* 40

iii. *Godwin and Godwinism* . . *Page* 57

iv. 1793 . . . . . *Page* 73

v. *Guilt and Sorrow : The Borderers* . . . . *Page* 82

vi. Elements . . . . *Page* 94

vii. Eyes and Ears . . . *Page* 102

viii. The 'Immortal Ode' . . *Page* 112

ix. Sense and Imagination . . *Page* 125

x. 'The Waters Sleep' . . *Page* 136

xi. The Preface to *Lyrical Ballads*. *Page* 143

xii. The Composition of *The Prelude* . . . . . *Page* 186

xiii. Dorothy Wordsworth . . *Page* 212

Alas! the sanctities combined
By art to unsensualize the mind
Decay and languish; or, as creeds
And humours change, are spurned like weeds:
The priests are from their altars thrust;
Temples are levelled with the dust;
And solemn rites and awful forms
Founder amid fanatic storms.

i
BIOGRAPHY AND AUTOBIOGRAPHY

It is often said that poetry is its own interpretation—or it is bad poetry. Such a way of speaking is at once plausible and fashionable, seeming as it does to lift the criticism of poetry into an ideal region uninfected by the infirmities of the personal judgement. Yet a man's poetry is but a part of him. A book, whatever its genius, is only the fragment of a wider effort; a wandering meteorite, flung off from the unconjectured path of a luminary distant and mysterious; no more, often, than—as it were—the frigescent débris of a once glowing totality of inspiration. The falling star, unrelatedly precipitant, is neither articulate nor intelligible; nor in books is there such a thing as perfectly adequate human speech, nor are our ears always, or ever, perfectly attuned to the perception of style.

I say this with reference to the proper limits, in criticism, of our interest in the lives of the poets. A poet endeavours to teach, to say something; and we to understand him. He has not said—in the nature of things, he could not say—all that he wished to say; nor any part of it wholly as he wished it said. Man and book are together a single effect; and it is, surely, the very pedantry of criticism—it is mere 'bookishness'—when the poet stands by, to put him out of the room. After all, if we put the poet out of the room, we invariably let in one of two interlopers. We let in either ourselves or a false image of the poet. We let in ourselves because we bring to our reading always our own preconceptions, our own personality and experience, and something of the collective experience of the age in which we live. No poem of Wordsworth will ever mean to any one to-day quite what it meant to Coleridge or Hazlitt; and any two persons to-day will differ from one another in their conception of it by a difference only less wide than that which separates both of them from Coleridge and Hazlitt. We can never be wholly exempt from this confusion; but the surest safeguard which we can have against the intrusion of our own personality is a close acquaintance with that of our poet. Of the degree to which, even where we are most successful in shutting out ourselves, we replace the poet by a false image of him (whencesoever derived), Wordsworth himself is the best possible illustration. For something like a century the understanding of his poetry has been vitiated by the presence of the false image which Fitzgerald christened ' Daddy Wordsworth '.

I propose accordingly to consider the poetry of Wordsworth in rather close connexion with his life; and upon the whole I am content to defend the method simply upon the ground of its naturalness. After all, is anything more desirable than that we should look at poetry in as natural a fashion as possible? I owe it, however, to the reader to say at once that I shall treat only a part of the poetry of Wordsworth, and that I shall not attempt the construction of a systematic biography. Moreover, in speaking of the poems, I shall adhere to interpretation, and eschew literary criticism in its larger sense. I shall not stray, that is, outside interpretation, into the wider and pleasanter field of appreciation. Appreciation commonly follows understanding;

and it certainly lags where understanding lags. If any one thinks that Wordsworth is easy to understand, I shall hope to persuade him that it is not so. No poet, perhaps, can be easy who is so essentially and pervasively subjective. But apart from that, it must be remembered that Wordsworth is the most theoretical of poets. He is doubly theoretical: all that he ever wrote proceeded, not only from a theory of poetry, but from a theory of life. He wished, as he said, to be regarded as a teacher or as nothing; and his teaching has its basis, not only in a definite metaphysic, a particular conception of the human mind and of the external world, but also in a defined view as to the place of man in society. For myself, I am inclined to think that, if we leave aside poets who, like Pindar, are difficult on purpose, or who, like Browning, are difficult because they are impatient of delay, we shall find Wordsworth one of the hardest of poets. And he is often hardest where he is best.

In what follows, then, I propose no more than to try and *understand* certain portions of Wordsworth's best work. Wordsworth began writing poetry, like everybody else, at the age of fourteen. But, unlike most people, he continued the practice of it for no less than sixty-six years afterwards. In so doing he set to the world a problem which it will be one of my objects, in the pages that follow, to elucidate. Nearly everything by which Wordsworth is supreme was written in a single decade of his life, in the period between 1797 and 1807. Outside these limits he wrote, of course, much that was interesting; but almost nothing that could bring him into the very first rank of poets, almost nothing that was of a piece with the splendid achievement of the *decas mirabilis*. Any one who has in his

LYRICAL BALLADS,

WITH

OTHER POEMS.

IN TWO VOLUMES.

By W. WORDSWORTH.

Quam nihil ad genium, Papiniane, tuum!

VOL. I.

SECOND EDITION.

LONDON:

PRINTED FOR T. N. LONGMAN AND O. REES, PATERNOSTER-ROW,

BY BIGGS AND CO. BRISTOL.

1800.

LYRICAL BALLADS,

WITH

OTHER POEMS.

IN TWO VOLUMES.

By W. WORDSWORTH.

Quam nihil ad genium, Papiniane, tuum!

VOL. II.

LONDON:

PRINTED FOR T. N. LONGMAN AND O. REES, PATERNOSTER-ROW,
BY BIGGS AND CO. BRISTOL.
1800.

hands *Lyrical Ballads*,[1] the *Poems in Two Volumes* of 1807, and the *Prelude* (which, though published posthumously, belongs to the same period), has before him the best of Wordsworth. He has before him nearly all of Wordsworth that is supreme, and very little of that part of him which one would wish away. These three books together form, as it were, an oasis of power and splendour amid endless arid tracts of middling performance.[2] The phenomenon is one to which I know no real parallel in literary history. It was remarked by Matthew Arnold, and, no doubt, before him. But I do not know that any one has seriously sought an explanation of it. The most commonly current explanation of it I take to be that which connects the failure of Wordsworth's poetical power with the collapse of the ideas which gave birth to (or were born of) the French Revolution. The French Revolution, it is supposed, made Wordsworth a great poet; and he continued to be a great poet just so long as he drew inspiration from the Revolutionary Idea. It is perhaps a question whether literary criticism has not become somewhat too much habituated to seeing all things in the French Revolution—as Malebranche saw all things in God (and too much habituated, it may be, to interpreting literature generally by political and social environment). Undoubtedly the French Revolution deeply influenced Wordsworth; and to understand the exact nature of this influence is a primary duty of the student of Wordsworth. But it is a duty which is sometimes, I fancy, discharged in a superficial

---

[1] In the second edition (1800). This adds to the edition of 1798 thirty-eight new poems (all written in the years 1799–1800).

[2] To the books mentioned should be added that portion of the *Excursion* which contains the story of Margaret (1799), and the posthumously published fragment of *The Recluse* (1800).

POEMS,

IN

TWO VOLUMES,

BY

WILLIAM WORDSWORTH,

AUTHOR OF

THE LYRICAL BALLADS.

Posterius graviore sono tibi Musa loquetur
Nostra: dabunt cum securos mihi tempora fructus.

VOL. I.

LONDON:

PRINTED FOR LONGMAN, HURST, REES, AND ORME,
PATERNOSTER-ROW.

1807.

fashion, and with an odd failure to make distinctions which are of real importance.

I propose, then, to take up the consideration of Wordsworth's poetry at that point at which it first connects with the French Revolution, and to follow its development as far as the year 1807. And in doing so, I shall pursue, as I have indicated, a method somewhat closely biographical. Wordsworth himself, in his old age, deprecated the design of a formal narrative of his life.[1] The impenetrable reserve of Homer and Shakespeare did not deter him from the paradox that the lives of the poets are sufficiently written in their poetry. As the pledge of his paradox, he has left us the *Prelude*. Yet he can hardly have supposed that posterity would be content to let the matter rest there; and even when, in his last years, he dictated a short autobiographical memoir (together with what are known as the Fenwick Notes), he was scarcely ignorant that there is no measure to the curiosity which greatness excites.

It was otherwise with his first biographer, his nephew, Bishop Christopher Wordsworth. The bishop understood, it is to be supposed, neither greatness nor the inquisitive zeal of its votaries. A recent critic[2] has charged him roundly with an unworthy reticence. It would perhaps be fairer to him to say that he conceived the grandeur of life to consist in its decorum, and the art of biography to be realized in edification. That there was a moral obligation upon him to wash in public the dirty linen of a family nearly connected with the English episcopate, neither temperament nor education had

---

[1] C. Wordsworth, *Memoirs*, i, p. 1. Wordsworth had perhaps taken fright at De Quincey's *Reminiscences*.
[2] Harper, *Wordsworth*, i, pp. 126–7

Biography and Autobiography

fitted him to perceive: nor, indeed, the conditions of his age—for he wrote half a century before the Golden Age of Vulgarity. Yet it is likely that a man of larger temperament, and of a finer literary tact, could have said, upon matters where to say something was vital, a great deal more than he did say. The fact is that 'Dulness and Fate' called Bishop Wordsworth, as it has summoned more loudly better men, to an office for the adequate discharge of which there was needed greater art than he possessed. It is easy to call his book disingenuous; but it is juster to observe that to perfectly ingenuous writing there must go (what Bishop Wordsworth could not bring) a considerable degree of cleverness. It is proper to call the book merely dull. It may even be said to be dull beyond excuse. Lowell[1] is not unjust to it when he says that its author ' has encumbered the memory of his uncle with two volumes of *Memoirs* which, for confused dreariness, are only matched by the Rev. Mark Noble's *History of the Protectorate House of Cromwell* '—one need not know both terms of the comparison to appreciate its justice. It is true that the *Memoirs* are praised by Professor Knight. But we may take this praise to be either the formal magnanimity of a second-in-the-field towards his predecessor, or else the sober tolerance of one not himself sure of success in a difficult business which has already bred one patent failure. No serious student of Wordsworth would wish to speak disrespectfully of Professor Knight. Yet a student of Wordsworth would cease to be serious if he pretended that Professor Knight's three volumes of biography either satisfied him or did not sate him. They furnish not a narrative,

[1] *Literary Essays*, iv, p. 388.

but the material for one; and even so they treat cursorily and superficially that part of Wordsworth's life which is most interesting—his early period—and with a minute and tedious conscientiousness his uninspired middle age and old age. They attempt, again, a rigid separation between the office of the biographer and that of the literary critic. In this severe demarcation of functions there is, as I have hinted, something contrary to nature; and in literature, as in life, nature mostly takes her revenge on those who affront her. On Professor Knight she has perhaps revenged herself too heavily—she has in fact passed his inheritance to others.

The authoritative life of Wordsworth is now that of Mr. Harper.[1] That such a work should come to us from an American scholar is perhaps not without its fitness. Wordsworth, at any rate in his later years, entertained no very favourable opinion of American customs and institutions. In this he was not a little ungrateful. Lowell has pointed out that Wordsworth was appreciated in America some time before he was tolerated in England. As early as 1802 there was a sufficient list of American subscribers to encourage a publisher in Philadelphia to produce an edition of *Lyrical Ballads*. Readers of Wordsworth's letters, again, will recall that among his correspondents was Professor Reed, a discriminating editor who did much to make him known in the United States. Emerson also was one of Wordsworth's earliest admirers, making two pilgrimages to Rydal Mount (in 1833 and 1848), of which he has left

[1] *William Wordsworth: His Life, Works, and Influence.* Mr. Harper's book was published in 1916, but somewhat side-tracked by the War. A supplement to it, *Wordsworth's French Daughter*, appeared in 1921.

a brief record in *English Traits*. (If Emerson, however, was a Wordsworthian, Wordsworth, I am sorry to say, was very far from being an Emersonian—writing to Professor Reed in 1841 he speaks of Emerson's essays with an unmeasured severity.) I have already mentioned Lowell; and to him we owe one of the best appreciations of Wordsworth that exists. It is worth recalling also that it was to an American audience that Clough delivered his admirable, but neglected, lecture upon Wordsworth.[1] Mr. Harper, therefore, is part of a distinguished tradition. In the pages which follow I shall have occasion to speak often of his book (which may, indeed, be regarded as, in some sense, the cause of my own); and even where Mr. Harper is not named, a good deal of what I have to say will be in the nature of implicit criticism of his work. It is proper, therefore, that I should say here and at once a few words about the scope and character of Mr. Harper's book, and about those features of it which mark it off from other biographies of Wordsworth.

The dominant idea of his book Mr. Harper owes, confessedly, to a French scholar, M. Émile Legouis. Bishop Wordsworth, as I have said, elected, when he undertook the *Memoirs* to concentrate the whole weight of his dull and cautious mind upon the dull and cautious period of his uncle's life. Succeeding biographers followed his example, whether by choice or of necessity. From M. Legouis came the first attempt to redress the balance; and his *Jeunesse de Wordsworth*, if a degree diffuse, may still be regarded as the best book upon Wordsworth that there is. In this book, for the first time, the whole emphasis is thrown where it should be,

[1] *Prose Remains*, pp. 305 sqq.

upon Wordsworth's youthful period. Herein Mr. Harper, though he deals with the life of Wordsworth in all its periods, is M. Legouis's disciple; and he has at the same time brought together a good deal of new material. The detail of this new material is, for the most part, disposed with judgement; and though in certain particulars it is not only new, but a little startling, Mr. Harper is sufficiently wise and happy in his scholarship to avoid sensationalism. The most startling item in this new material is by now fairly generally known. During his residence in France Wordsworth formed an attachment to a French girl, who bore the name Marie-Anne Vallon (the 'Annette' of the letters and journal of Dorothy Wordsworth). Everybody knows the sonnet of Wordsworth composed upon the beach of Calais in 1802, the sonnet beginning 'It is a beauteous evening calm and free'. The girl addressed in the latter part of the poem, in the lines 'Dear child, dear girl, that walkest with me here', was a daughter of Wordsworth and Marie-Anne Vallon. Let us agree that this is startling, and that it compels us to look at Wordsworth in a new way. But it is not necessary that we should lose our heads; nor do I think that Mr. Harper has lost his head. Nor, I think, will any reasonable person complain of him for disinterring facts about Wordsworth's private life which previous biographers buried —stupidly and timorously. It must needs be that there should be small talk about great men; and after all, the impertinence of our curiosity is, as a rule, fairly proportioned to the greatness of its object. Certainly there is a point of fame when we make both poetry and criticism ridiculous if we persist in regarding the relation between a poet and his reader as that between one gentleman and another. The poet is thought of as a man who writes a book. The book that he writes is his poetry. He gives you that (he, in fact, sells it to you), and you have no right, it is urged, to follow him home. I think it would be at least as true to say that a poet is a man who throws a stone at your window (if he is a poet of any power he breaks it). You run to the window, or you pursue him down the street, because you, quite properly, want to know something more about him than the stone. A great poet is not an ordinary occurrence. We must not class the advent of great poetry with the daily delivery of the milk and the bread. A great poet is a challenge; and he must abide our question. He may, no doubt, claim certain reserves; just as he claims copyright—and perhaps for about the same period. But that even for that period he can claim every kind of reserve (or that others can claim it for him), I should be tempted to question. In general I should be inclined to say that we are entitled to all the talk, small and great, about great poets, which we can scrape together, with this proviso: that we can, and do, relate it to the primary fact about them, namely that they *are* great. Mr. Harper, I think, on the whole gives heed to this proviso. Yet he appears to me not altogether to have escaped a different kind of extravagance. In writing his life of Wordsworth he set out, as I surmise, to kill a conception of Wordsworth which was certainly false, and to which I have already alluded: the conception propagated by the official biographies and crystallized by Fitzgerald in the phrase 'Daddy Wordsworth'. He conceived that, if he could replace this conception by the image of a Wordsworth rather more like Byron or Burns, he could do the poet a genuine service. Wordsworth could be saved by being relieved of his oppressive respectability. There was a period in which Wordsworth was a republican (a less respectable thing than it is now, and certainly not a thing to keep, or advertise, in an episcopal family); a republican, a pacifist, a disciple of Godwin, a necessitarian, a 'semi-atheist', a youth cast off by his relations, an object of suspicion to Government spies and good men generally, lax in moral principle and practice. It is this period to which Mr. Harper looks, I will not say for the true Wordsworth, but for the Wordsworth who matters. It was this environment that made him. It is this that explains him.

No! It is this that makes him need explanation. Mr. Harper seems to me first of all to have confused the statement of the problem with its solution, and then, in a natural enthusiasm, to have given to the statement of it an exaggerated form. The reaction from the old official biographies of Wordsworth is, no doubt, healthy. But we must not allow it to carry us to an extreme equally vicious. The Byronic Wordsworth is on the whole more untrue, I believe, than 'Daddy Wordsworth'. In both the life and the mind of Wordsworth there is a somewhat prolonged period of conflict, the fact and the significance of which have hitherto not been adequately regarded. We have been too long and too much in the habit of regarding Wordsworth as belonging wholly and essentially to the order of sabbatical men, too prone to 'fancy that the mighty deep was even the gentlest of all gentle things'. We have associated him too exclusively with that 'harmony' and that 'deep power of joy' which belongs to his supreme period. It is salutary to be reminded that this sabbatical calm was not a talent, but a conquest. Behind it is conflict.

Yet we are only using loose language when, in this or any analogous connexion, we say that the real man is seen in the conflict. The real man is seen, not in the conflict, but in the issue of the conflict. When the conflict has found its issue, we usually discover that many incidents of it which seemed of primary importance possess really an interest which is secondary or altogether negligible.

Undoubtedly Mr. Harper's book puts to us a good deal in the life of Wordsworth which, in Wordsworth's own account of himself, is passed over either lightly or in complete silence. Mr. Harper finds in the *Prelude* a considerable degree of confusion and contradiction—in particular he feels that Wordsworth reads back into his early period some of the opinions and sentiments of his later years. Which of us does not? And he is clearly at times uneasy over some of Wordsworth's reserves. Yet upon the whole I take it that he would be as little inclined as I am myself to think of the *Prelude* as an untruthful or disingenuous book. For myself, Mr. Harper's book sent me back to the *Prelude*—and no doubt it did the same service for a great many other persons. I hope it is no disrespect to Mr. Harper to say that I rose from the re-reading of the *Prelude* with the sense that Wordsworth understood himself, not only better than Mr. Harper would have us suppose, but better than Mr. Harper has understood him—that he had drawn the lines of his own life with a truer emphasis.

Wordsworth, in a letter to Sir George Beaumont, speaks of the composition of the *Prelude* as 'a thing unprecedented in literary history—that a man should write so much about himself'. Line for line, the *Prelude* is, perhaps, not so long as Gibbon's *Memoirs*, which appeared three years before the *Prelude* was begun; and it is a very modest undertaking by the side of Goethe's *Dichtung und Wahrheit*, which began to appear some six years after the *Prelude* was completed. On the other hand, an autobiographical poem almost as long as *Paradise Lost* is a notable enterprise for a young man of twenty-nine whose title to genius and repute rested on no more secure a foundation than the testimony of his own consciousness. When we remember that the author meditated a continuation which would have brought the dimensions of the whole somewhere near those, say, of the *Faerie Queene*, it may perhaps be called an alarming enterprise. It is true that it was the age of the egotists. It was an age in which the distinguishing mark of nearly every aspirant to poetical greatness was precisely that he wrote (and published) a history of his own soul. He did not always say that he was doing so; he did not necessarily offer, as Wordsworth in the *Prelude*, overt and confessed autobiography. But the paramount interest of each of the principal poets of the time was undoubtedly the history of his own mind. It is a commonplace that Byron is the hero of each of his more considerable poems. But the same absorbing egotism appears in Shelley. *Alastor* is a history of Shelley's soul: *Epipsychidion* is another. Equally truly, though less obviously, *Endymion* is a history of the soul of Keats. If one or two poets—as Southey—did not give the world histories of their souls, this was perhaps not want of will, but want of soul. Even Scott, the most refreshingly objective of poets, has left us in prose an autobiographic fragment pitched to a scale which attests a manly sense of his significance to the world.

The autobiographic habit seized Wordsworth at an

early age. ' I wrote ', he tells us, ' while yet a schoolboy, a long poem running upon my own adventures and the scenery of the country in which I was brought up.'[1] This poem, we are told in the Fenwick Notes, 'contained thoughts and images most of which ' were dispersed later through the poet's ' other writings '. No doubt, some of these ' thoughts and images ' have a place in the first two books of the *Prelude*. It must be further remembered that, if the passion for autobiography seized Wordsworth early, it did not leave him till a period considerably later than the date of the *Prelude*. The *Excursion* is hardly less autobiographic than the *Prelude*. Its nine books introduce us to three heroes; and each of them is Wordsworth himself. In particular, it is worth observing (I do not know that it has been hitherto observed) that the character of the *Solitary*, though, according to an express statement of Wordsworth himself,[2] it was drawn from ' a Mr. Fawcett, a preacher at a Dissenting meeting-house at the Old Jewry ', fills a gap in the account which, in the *Prelude*, Wordsworth gives of his own revolutionary period. The Wordsworth of Books IX–XI of the *Prelude* has just escaped being the *Solitary*. Wordsworth speaks of ' poor Fawcett ', and says of him patronizingly that ' like many others in those times of shewy talents, he had not strength of character to withstand the effects of the French Revolution, and of the wild and lax opinions which had done so much towards producing it '.[3] That is an ungenerous note. But it belongs to the last years of Wordsworth's life, when it was no longer wholly in his power either to remember truly or to feel freshly.

[1] Grosart, iii, p. 221.   [2] *Ib.*. pp. 197–8.   [3] *Loc. cit.*

'It is difficult for a man to speak long of himself', says Hume, 'without vanity.' In his private life Wordsworth was, there is reason to believe, both egotistical and vain. It is the more remarkable, therefore, that the *Prelude*, conceived in, and throughout informed by, a gigantesque egotism, is yet utterly devoid of vanity. It is mysteriously and divinely void, not only of vanity, but of pride. Gibbon, when he passes from the history of European civilization to the history of himself, becomes at once vulgar and absurd. Goethe, professing to put to us the 'Truth and Poetry' which nursed his greatness, must needs be both a bore and a snob. Even from Scott we have to tolerate that interminable pride of ancestry which so often dulls the edge of chivalrous and romantic minds. But the author of the *Prelude* was born, one might think, of a mountain or a river, rather than of human parents; and everything that he has to tell us of himself meets us like a clean breeze, carrying none of the casual impurities of social or intellectual competition.

The purpose of the poem is twofold; first, a self-examination, to discover how far the writer is indeed a poet, whether he is fit for work that can live; and, secondly, a self-expression, enfolding the expression of an age of renewed nobility of manners:

> May my life
> Express the image of a better time,
> More wise desires and simpler manners.

There you have the conscious language of the saints—only those speak thus who carry within them an inalienable assurance of their own poetic salvation. The lines I have quoted are written with deliberate reminiscence of Milton; and perhaps only Milton and Wordsworth voice

Biography and Autobiography

this assurance without absurdity. Both are consciously dedicated poets. 'Milton is his great idol', Hazlitt wrote, ' and he sometimes dares to compare himself with him.' The comparison, as Hazlitt quite well knew, was not so absurd as he would have us suppose; but it is Hazlitt's manner to mix always a spice of malice with his worship of the great poets his contemporaries. A certain Miltonic purity informs even those parts of the *Prelude* which are most wanting in Miltonic loftiness of style; and of the poem as a whole it may be said that it is built in and round that grandiose conception of the nature of the poetic art to which Milton has given, in *The Reason of Church Government*, immortal expression:

' a work not to be raised from the heat of youth, or the vapours of wine; like that which flows at waste from the pen of some vulgar amourist, or the trencher-fury of a rhyming parasite; nor to be obtained by the invocation of Dame Memory and her siren daughters, but by devout prayer to that eternal Spirit, who can enrich with all utterance and knowledge, and sends out his seraphim, with the hallowed fire of his altar to touch and purify the lips of whom he pleases.'

In the introduction to the *Prelude* Wordsworth speaks of himself plainly as ' a renovated spirit singled out . . . for holy services ', and of his verse as a ' priestly robe ' casting itself spontaneously about him (*Prelude*, i. 51–3). And again, in the fourth book, he tells us that a ' bond ' was given to him that he should be,

      else sinning greatly,
  A dedicated spirit.

The circumstances in which, in the latter of these two passages, the ' bond ' was given are not a little notable.

      I had passed
  The night in dancing, gaiety and mirth,

> With din of instruments and shuffling feet,
> And glancing forms and tapers glittering,
> And unaimed prattle flying up and down,
> Spirits upon the stretch, and here and there
> Slight shocks of young love-liking interspersed,
> Whose transient pleasure mounted to the head
> And tingled through the veins.

To the dance and prattle and love-liking succeeds, as the young poet finds his way home on foot, a 'memorable pomp' of dawn—laughing sea and shining hills and dew and mist and the melody of birds:

> My heart was full; I made no vows, but vows
> Were then made for me; bond unknown to me
> Was given that I should be, else sinning greatly,
> A dedicated spirit. On I walked
> In thankful blessedness, which yet survives.

To a good many persons there is some suggestion of the ludicrous in the image of a Wordsworth dancing and prattling and 'love-liking' (or, put plainly, flirting). But Wordsworth was always ready to be ludicrous for the purpose of being perfectly truthful; and there can, I think, be no doubt that, looking back into the past, he was vividly conscious of aspects of himself which his readers are apt to miss, or not sufficiently to pause upon. The opening of the sixth book recalls similarly 'nights of revelry' with the 'frank-hearted maids of rocky Cumberland' (vi. 13)—where the humourless gloss 'frank-hearted' deceives nobody nor was intended to deceive; and in many other passages he is at pains to emphasize that side of himself which corresponds with the normal youth of average young men. If the images which for this purpose he calls up seem to us at times incongruous, the incongruity was not missed by Wordsworth himself. Often, as he tells us, he felt as though he were describing some one other than himself :

> So wide appears
> The vacancy between me and those days
> Which yet have such self-presence in my mind,
> That, musing on them, often do I seem
> Two consciousnesses, conscious of myself
> And of some other being.

The purpose of the *Prelude* may, indeed, be said to be to search out and seize and hold, among the many seemingly alien and incongruous images of self cast up by reflection, the image of the poet's true being, of his slowly self-realizing individuality, of that in him in virtue of which he is a ' dedicated spirit '. The ' Preamble ' to the *Prelude* (i.e. i. 1-45) was written (probably) in 1795; and the conclusion of the poem carries the narrative of the poet's life down to the date of the ' Preamble '. But apart from the ' Preamble ', the work dates from 1799-1800[1]; and the conditions out of which it arose deserve attention. Wordsworth settled in Grasmere with his sister towards the close of 1799. Coleridge came to Grasmere in the spring of 1800. The *Prelude* is dedicated to him. The first two books were completed in 1800 under the stimulus of his presence. Thereafter the whole was laid aside for four years ; and the work resumed, in view of his impending departure, in the spring of 1804. The poem was finished off against his return by the end of 1806. It may be said, I think, throughout to have been written to him and for him—and in a sense *by* him. In this poem, and elsewhere, Coleridge may fairly be thought of as the guardian angel

[1] See, however, the essay upon the Composition of *The Prelude*, pp. 186 sqq., where a somewhat different dating is tentatively suggested.

of Wordsworth's poetical genius. Perhaps, indeed, Coleridge's greatest work is Wordsworth—and, like all his other work, Coleridge left it unfinished. If there was any medicine for the decline of power which stole over Wordsworth's poetry after 1807, it was perhaps to be sought from Coleridge. From Coleridge Wordsworth had derived the elements of his metaphysic; and his genius died of a metaphysical atrophy. It is hardly an accident that the period of the decline of power coincides with the period in which Wordsworth's gradual estrangement from Coleridge began.[1]

When Coleridge joined the Wordsworths in Westmorland in 1800, both poets were full of ambitious projects. The opening portion of the first book of the *Prelude* enumerates some of the large themes of poetry which were passing through Wordsworth's mind. But in respect of all of them he was conscious of

Impediments from day to day renewed. (i. 131.)

Everywhere he found either some defect in the theme or in his own powers; and his genius began to 'recoil and droop and seek repose in listlessness' (i. 265–6).

This is the moment of the *Prelude*. He feels himself to be

Unprofitably travelling toward the grave. (i. 267.)

Was it for this, he asks, that he was born in sound of Derwent water, and cradled amid lake and mountain? (i. 269 sqq.).

The transition to autobiography is made with splendid ease and naturalness; and the remaining portion of the

[1] The dependence upon Coleridge is well illustrated, as late as 1805, by a letter of Wordsworth to Beaumont, with reference to the *Recluse*: 'Should Coleridge return', Wordsworth writes, 'so that I might have some conversation with him, I should go on swimmingly' (*Letters*, i, p. 196).

Biography and Autobiography

first book contains effects of poetry hardly surpassed in our literature. But they are effects educed from material strangely commonplace and unpromising. It is worth while to tabulate this material. It is made up of eight themes:

> Bathing.
> Bird-snaring.
> Birds-nesting.
> An expedition in a stolen boat.
> Skating.
> Fishing.
> Kite-sailing.
> Noughts-and-crosses and cards.

Under these eight themes Wordsworth disposes the history of his childhood till the age of ten. These eight images of himself surge up on the main stream of memory: images, as might seem, of a self very ordinary and not very interesting. But the true comment upon them may be found in a later book of the *Prelude*:

> O mystery of man, from what a depth
> Proceed thy honours. I am lost, but see
> In simple childhood something of the base
> On which thy greatness stands. . . .
> . . . The days gone by
> Return upon me almost from the dawn
> Of life: the hiding-places of man's power
> Open. (xii. 272 sqq.)

Of the philosophic implications of this comment I shall have something to say later. Here I will content myself with illustrating, by a single example, the kind of power which Wordsworth brings to bear upon his oddly selected themes. Here is his account of the Expedition in the Stolen Boat (i. 356–400):

One summer evening, led by her,[1] I found
A little boat tied to a willow tree
Within a rocky cave, its usual home.
Straight I unloosed her chain, and stepping in
Pushed from the shore. It was an act of stealth
And troubled pleasure; nor without the voice
Of mountain echoes did my boat move on;
Leaving behind her still, on either side,
Small circles glittering idly in the moon,
Until they melted all into one track
Of sparkling light. But now, like one who rows,
Proud of his skill, to reach a chosen point
With an unswerving line, I fixed my view
Upon the summit of a craggy ridge,
The horizon's utmost boundary; far above
Was nothing but the stars and the grey sky.
She was an elfin pinnace; lustily
I dipped my oars into the silent lake,
And, as I rose upon the stroke, my boat
Went heaving through the water like a swan;
When, from behind that craggy steep till then
The horizon's bound, a huge peak, black and huge,
As if with voluntary power instinct
Upreared its head. I struck and struck again,
And growing still in stature the grim shape
Towered up between me and the stars, and still,
For so it seemed, with purpose of its own
And measured motion like a living thing
Strode after me. With trembling oars I turned,
And through the silent water stole my way
Back to the covert of the willow tree;
There in her mooring-place I left my bark,—
And through the meadows homeward went, in grave
And serious mood; but after I had seen
That spectacle, for many days my brain
Worked with a dim and undetermined sense
Of unknown modes of being; o'er my thoughts
There hung a darkness, call it solitude

[1] i.e. led by Nature.

> Or blank desertion. No familiar shapes
> Remained, no pleasant images of trees,
> Of sea or sky, no colours of green fields;
> But huge and mighty forms, that do not live,[1]
> Like living men moved slowly through the mind
> By day, and were a trouble to my dreams.

There follows immediately the well-known apostrophe to the ' Wisdom and Spirit of the Universe ', which, from the first dawn of childhood, has ' not in vain ' bound the poet's ' human soul ' to ' high objects ' and ' enduring things ', using him to find even thus early

> A grandeur in the beatings of the heart.

During the period covered by the first book, the first ten years of childhood, this Wisdom and Spirit has been ' intervenient ' only; as it were, casually solemnizing the animal happiness of childhood. The second book conducts us to a second stage in the relation of the child to Nature. The book begins with themes in appearance not less trivial than those which fill Book I: boating, riding excursions, bowling. But in this second period (covering the ages of ten to seventeen) Nature, no longer ' intervenient ' merely, is consciously sought. She is sought because, from her earlier ' interveniences ', she has become associated with happiness. She has become so associated, not merely in connexion with the purely animal happinesses which have already been enumerated, but in connexion with the happiness of the human affections. By the time that he was thirteen Wordsworth had lost both his father and his mother. He notices how, in the case of all children, their first introduction to the objects of the natural world comes

---

[1] I have corrected here an obviously false punctuation. The editions have no comma after *live,* but place one after *living men.*

through their parents. Now 'the props of my affection were removed', he says (ii. 279). But the world of nature which these props had sustained for him abided in its strength:

> I was left alone
> Seeking the visible world, nor knowing why.
> The props of my affections were removed;
> And yet the building stood, as if sustained
> By its own spirit.

Of his relation to natural influences in this second period Wordsworth offers an account somewhat more analytic than that given of the first period. Nature is now primary. He 'walks with nature' in 'the spirit of religious love'; and he conceives his communion with her to be (and indeed to have been in the earlier period) a condition, not merely passive, but creative:

> I still retained
> My first creative sensibility.

The senses are, in fact, for Wordsworth, from the beginning creative. This is a doctrine to which we shall have occasion to recur. Here it may suffice to call attention to an element in his experience of Nature to which the second book of the *Prelude* affords the first clear testimony. From his childhood it was a common happening that, in his contemplation of the external world, the object contemplated lost its dependence upon sense-perception—its externality fell away: bodily eyes, he says,

> bodily eyes
> Were utterly forgotten, and what I saw
> Appeared like something in myself, a dream,
> A prospect in the mind.

The lines should be interpreted in connexion with a

passage in the Fenwick Notes. Speaking there of the great *Ode*, Wordsworth says:

' I was often unable to think of external things as having external existence, and I communed with all that I saw as something not apart from, but inherent in, my own immaterial nature. Many times while going to school have I grasped a wall or tree to recall myself from this abyss of idealism to the reality. . . . To that dreamlike vividness and splendour which invest objects of sight in childhood every one, I believe, if he would look back, could bear testimony.' (Grosart, iii, p. 195.)

It is no doubt true that analogous experiences may be attested by the consciousness even of commonplace persons. Now and again each of us is a god. But these experiences, occasional and weak in other men, are with Wordsworth strong and constant. It is these, and experiences congenial with them, that make his life. It is in virtue of these that he knows himself, as he calls up in the *Prelude* the pageant of images which make his past, to be ' a dedicated spirit '. The *Prelude* is, in fact, the history of a consciousness highly abnormal; and it is only in proportion as we realize this, that we can understand either Wordsworth himself or his poetry. Wordsworth himself has done something to confuse us. Serenely conscious as he is of his ' dedicated ' character, and connecting this as he does, in the *Prelude* and elsewhere, with what his childhood intimated of immortality, he is none the less apt to deduce his own experience of Nature from something common to himself and to ordinary men. And this carries, for his art, a curious corollary. Very often (more often than any other poet) Wordsworth writes as ordinary men write—that is to say, unpoetically.

The second book of the *Prelude* carries us to Words-

worth's seventeenth year. It closes the period of what
may be called purely internal biography. Thus far he
had had little contact with, and had made very little
reflection upon, men and man's nature. To the seclusion
of his earliest years he traces two benefits. In the first
place, for a longer period than most youths, he had
enjoyed an experience of the natural world in which
the free creative activity of the senses was not impeded
or deadened by custom and convention. 'By the
regular action of the world', he says, 'my soul was
unsubdued' (ii. 361–2). Secondly, such acquaintance
as he had made with man had been so conditioned
that the form of man appeared always against a back-
ground of what was pure or solemn or sublime. The
far-reaching consequences of this accident are developed
in the 'Retrospect' of Book VIII of the *Prelude*:

> A rambling schoolboy, thus
> I felt his presence in his own domain,
> As of a lord and master, or a power,
> Or genius, under nature, under God,
> Presiding; and severest solitude
> Had more commanding looks when he was there.
> When up the lonely brooks on rainy days
> Angling I went, or trod the trackless hills
> By mists bewildered, suddenly mine eyes
> Have glanced upon him distant a few steps,
> In size a giant, stalking through thick fog,
> His sheep like Greenland bears; or, as he stepped
> Beyond the boundary-line of some hill-shadow,
> His form hath flashed upon me, glorified
> By the deep radiance of the setting sun:
> Or him have I descried in distant sky,
> A solitary object and sublime,
> Above all height! like an aerial cross
> Stationed alone upon a spiry rock
> Of the Chartreuse, for worship. Thus was man

> Ennobled outwardly before my sight,
> And thus my heart was early introduced
> To an unconscious love and reverence
> Of human nature.   (viii. 256 sqq.)

The four books which follow (III–VI) are occupied with the period during which Wordsworth was an undergraduate at Cambridge. Their themes are handled diffusely; and Wordsworth is commonly diffuse, I fancy, where he is exercising reserve and caution. This, and some other characters of the narrative, suggest the suspicion that it was a good deal revised in later years.[1] Uninforming as these books ultimately are, it will be felt, I think, if they are read carefully, that the period was one upon which Wordsworth looked back with an uncommon dissatisfaction and concern. 'I was not for that hour, Nor for that place,'[2] he says. The chief blessing of the period was that he carried within him 'independent solaces',

> To mitigate the injurious sway of place
> Or circumstance;   (iii. 101–3.)

solaces derived from his habit of communion with Nature. He was able, and often willing, to turn his mind 'upon

---

[1] Wordsworth protests repeatedly that the unprofitableness of his Cambridge period was due to himself, not the place (see particularly vi. 188–9). But the more he does so, the more I seem to myself to catch the accents, not of the Wordsworth of 1804, but of the Wordsworth whose brother was Master of Trinity. Other indications of a late revision are such passages as 610 sqq.:

> I cannot say what portion is in truth
> The naked recollection of that time,
> And what may rather have been called to life
> By after meditation;

the reference at 300 to 'the recreant age we live in'; and the occasional pietism which mars, e. g. 83–121.

[2] iii, 81–2.

itself', away from the vanity alike of youth and age, of ignorance and learning. It is an odd comment upon the benefits of university education; and it is expressed with a mildness which makes it more severe than the unsparing criticisms of, say, Gibbon. The terms were spent in idleness [1] or listlessness; the vacations, for the most part, in the dancing, revelry, and 'love-liking' which we have already had occasion to note (not without a 'shock of mild surprise'). Of any deeper unsettlement of mind or habit, nothing is said. In later life he told Lady Richardson that 'after he had finished his College course' he was conscious of a 'struggle between his conscience and his impulses' which made it impossible for him to enter the Church. Oddly enough (and yet, perhaps, not oddly, in the light of our better knowledge of him) he 'thought of a military life': 'he always fancied that he had talents for command'.[2] To the close of the period belongs his first serious preoccupation with literary composition.

> Those were the days
> Which also first emboldened me to trust
> With firmness, hitherto but slightly touched
> By such a daring thought, that I might leave
> Some monument behind me which pure hearts
> Should reverence.   (vi. 52 sqq.)

The time-reference is vague. But the allusion is, pretty clearly, to the poem entitled *An Evening Walk*, which we know to have been begun in 1787 (Wordsworth's first year in Cambridge) and finished probably

---

[1] Book V is devoted to the subject of reading. But it is not illuminating for the poet's own studies. The only books specifically mentioned are *Don Quixote* and the *Arabian Nights*, and these belong to the period of childhood.

[2] Grosart, iii, pp. 451–2.

Biography and Autobiography

in 1789 (the second year of the Cambridge period).[1] Of this piece it is beside my purpose to speak in detail. Compared with *Descriptive Sketches* (both poems were published in the same year, 1793),[2] the earlier composition is both more faulty—with the same species of faultiness—and less interesting. Its diction is derivative, and from sources mostly impure. Its versification (it is written in heroic couplets) neither is, nor could be, apt: the claims of 'point' are bullied and over-ridden by the demands of an impertinent talent for diffuse description. The only merit of the poem is that which Wordsworth himself emphasizes in the Fenwick Notes. Many of the 'images' (all, says Wordsworth himself) have been actually 'observed'.[3] Perhaps the only remarkable circumstance in connexion with it is that (together with *Descriptive Sketches*) it was enthusiastically received by the first Wordsworth Society which ever met. 'Coleridge', writes Chr. Wordsworth, in November 1793, 'spoke of the esteem in which my brother was holden by a society at Exeter.'[4] Perhaps even this ceases to be remarkable when it appears that the Exeter society had, among the other gods of its idolatry, Erasmus Darwin and Miss Seward.

[1] Wordsworth says: 'It was composed at school, and during my first two College [Long] vacations' (Grosart, iii, p. 4).

[2] They were reviewed together in *The Monthly Review* for October 1793. It does not seem to be generally known that the reviewer was Thomas Holcroft. (The Bodleian Library possesses the office copy of the *Monthly Review* in which the editor wrote in the names of each contributor. Holcroft—despite the *D. N. B.*—was a frequent contributor.)

[3] Grosart, *loc. cit.*

[4] *Social Life in the English Universities in the Eighteenth Century*, p. 589.

'DESCRIPTIVE SKETCHES'

THE supreme period of Wordsworth's art is, as I have said, the great decade 1797–1807. The interesting, the intriguing, period, is the formative period lying behind this, the five years of storm and stress which were the crisis of the poet's moral and intellectual development. The poetry of these five years is neither considerable in amount nor great in quality. But as a part of literary history it is of first-rate interest; and an understanding of it is essential to a just appreciation of Wordsworth's later and greater work. Three poems only come into consideration. They are, firstly, *Descriptive Sketches*, completed in the autumn of 1792, when Wordsworth was at the height of his revolutionary ardour; secondly, *Guilt and Sorrow*, finished in 1794; and thirdly, the dramatic poem of the *Borderers*, finished in 1796. In what follows I shall attempt an examination of these three poems, and of the circumstances out of which they arose, using the relevant portions of the *Prelude* as a kind of line-for-line commentary upon them. But I will make here one or two prefatory remarks of a general character which may, I hope, serve as guiding lines for the subsequent detailed examination.

Descriptive Sketches was written when Wordsworth was actually in France, and among the moving scenes of the first act of the Revolution: when he had thoughts of throwing in his lot actively with the leaders of the Girondist party. It is in fact, as will appear presently, the only poem which he wrote in what I may call the full faith of the French Revolution. And yet it is, of all his poems, with the exception of *An Evening Walk*, the most artificial, the least like anything that he wrote subsequently, the most like everything that was worst in the conventional manner of the latter part of the eighteenth century. I say that it is the only poem which he wrote in the full faith of the French Revolution; and if, in doing so, I say something that needs explanation, it is something also which deserves emphasis. No doubt both *Guilt and Sorrow* and the *Borderers* reflect strongly the revolutionary temper. They breathe revolution. But not the French Revolution. The pure air of the French Revolution is in both poems infected through and through with the mists of English political theory. The book of the moment was the *Political Justice* of William Godwin—a work of immense influence in its generation, and of which I shall have a good deal to say later. Godwin is written across every page of both *Guilt and Sorrow* and the *Borderers*; and the paradox of Godwin is that he is a revolutionary who does not believe in revolution. The aim of the French Revolution was to replace the arbitrary will of despotism and aristocracy by what Rousseau had called the 'general will'. To Godwin the 'general will' is the source of all evil. In 1792 Wordsworth saw everything in the French Revolution: in 1795 he tended to see everything in Godwin. He was, in fact, in 1795 in revolt against the French Revolution, and was enrolling himself betimes as the disciple of an extreme individualism: an individualism to which any government was necessarily the antithesis of the good, any organized expression of the 'general will' merely an obstacle to the perfectibility of the individual.

I put all this now dogmatically and elliptically; and I shall endeavour to amplify it as we proceed. It is necessary to put it thus in the foreground, not only because Wordsworth himself (if we read the *Prelude* attentively) does so, but because it enables us to seize a distinction which is not unimportant, and which, as I have hinted already, seems sometimes to be missed by those who suppose Wordsworth, in his great period, to have drawn his strength and inspiration from the French Revolution. The strength of Wordsworth's supreme period is, in fact, not the Revolutionary Idea, but his own reaction, first upon the failure of that Idea, and then upon the failure of Godwinism. I may illustrate this here and now from a letter of Coleridge. Writing to Wordsworth in 1799, Coleridge urges him to 'write a poem in blank verse, addressed to those who, in consequence of the complete failure of the French Revolution, have thrown up all hope of the amelioration of mankind'. M. Legouis has rightly brought this letter into connexion with the concluding portion of the second book of the *Prelude* (written in 1800). If in these times, Wordsworth there says,

>   If in these times of fear,
> This melancholy waste of hopes o'erthrown . . .[1]
>   . . . if in this time
> Of dereliction and dismay, I yet
> Despair not of our nature, but retain
> A more than Roman confidence,[2] a faith
> That fails not, in all sorrow my support . . .
>   . . . the gift is yours,
> Ye winds and sounding cataracts; 'tis yours,

---

[1] i.e. the hopes of the French Revolution.

[2] The phrase is not chosen at random; but has a specific reference to the rather showy Stoicism of the Godwinian philosophy.

> Ye mountains; thine, O Nature. Thou hast fed
> My lofty speculations, and in thee,
> For this uneasy heart of ours, I find
> A never-failing principle of joy
> And purest passion. (ii. 432 sqq.)

The whole effort, and the whole success, of Wordsworth's poetry during what I call his supreme decade is to bring to men disillusioned by the failure of the Revolutionary Idea the secret of a 'principle of joy' in the universe, 'a faith that fails not in all sorrow', a victory that lives in the very heart of defeat. The process by which he reached this success, by which he attained the discovery of this 'principle of joy', is obscurely related in the *Prelude*, with a good deal of deliberate, and admitted,[1] reserve, but on the whole with sufficient candour and clearness to enable us, with such external supplements as are available, to trace it in broad outline.

Descriptive Sketches, completed, as I have said, towards the close of 1792, was published in the early part of 1793. Its publication was synchronous with that of *An Evening Walk*. This synchronism, together with a similarity of style and versification between the two poems, has had the unfortunate effect of causing students of Wordsworth (or at any rate his casual readers) to regard them as proceeding from the same point of development. We know, however, from Wordsworth himself [2] that *An Evening Walk* was begun while he was still at

[1] See, especially, xi. 282 sqq.:

> Share with me, friend, the wish
> That some dramatic tale, endued with shapes
> Livelier, and flinging out *less guarded words*
> *Than suit the work we fashion,* might set forth
> What then I learned.

[2] See above, p. 39.

school, and finished during his first two years at college. Wordsworth went to France in November 1791, after completing his three years at Cambridge, and remained there until certainly December of the following year. Nearly the whole of *Descriptive Sketches*, he himself expressly tells us,[1] was composed upon the banks of the Loire during those thirteen months.

The poem, however, purports to describe a walking tour through France and Switzerland, which Wordsworth made, in company with an undergraduate friend of the name of Jones, in the summer of 1790. This long gap between incident and narrative marks the first emergence of a peculiarity in Wordsworth's method of composition which continued with him so long as he wrote poetry. At the very beginning of the *Prelude* he calls our attention to the fact that its opening paragraphs were contemporary with the feelings which they express—he wrote what he felt on the very day upon which he felt it. But he is curiously careful, in that passage, to explain to us that this was contrary to his usual method of composition. He speaks of himself as being 'not used to make A present joy the matter of a song'. Similarly in the Epilogue to the *Waggoner* he tells us that it was his habit to keep a theme in his mind for years before putting it into verse. He speaks of

> A shy spirit in my heart
> That comes and goes—will sometimes leap
> From hiding-places ten years deep,
> Or haunt me with familiar face,
> Returning like a ghost unlaid
> Until the debt I owe is paid.

We encounter here a doctrine which is part and parcel

[1] Grosart, iii, p. 7.

of Wordsworth's theory of poetic inspiration, and, as I hope to show later, of his theory of the relation between the mind and the senses. The theory has its formal expression in the preface to *Lyrical Ballads*. Poetry, we are there told, 'takes its origin from emotion recollected in tranquillity '.[1] Undoubtedly Wordsworth believed that this method reproduced with deeper truth the original impression. Aubrey de Vere reports a conversation with him in which he commends it, not as a method suitable merely to his own genius, but as of universal applicability. 'That which remained,' he said, ' the picture surviving in the mind, would have presented the ideal and essential truth of the scene, and done so in large part by discarding much which, though in itself striking, was not characteristic.' The discerning reader will not fail to observe here congruences with the teaching of Aristotle ; but he will perhaps—since it is but rarely that poets let us into their secrets of composition—be more interested in attending to Wordsworth's practice than to his theory. Wordsworth, as De Vere reports him, is speaking of the elimination of the unessential ; and, save perhaps by implication, he does not touch the question how far it is possible for the poet, under the conditions proposed for him, to avoid obtruding on his original impression the mental environment of the time of composition. The question is interesting, not only in connexion with *Descriptive Sketches* but also as affecting the problem of the essential truthfulness of large parts of the *Prelude*. It so happens that Wordsworth has described this Swiss tour twice

[1] Paragraph 23. In the essay upon the *Preface to Lyrical Ballads* I have attempted a detailed examination of this theory and its implications.

over; first in *Descriptive Sketches*, at a distance of two years, and subsequently, in a more partial fashion, in the sixth book of the *Prelude*. I have not space here (nor, perhaps, would it be relevant) to institute a detailed comparison of the two pieces. It will, however, be relevant (and will sufficiently hint wider theoretical implications) to show, as it can be shown, the essential untruthfulness of a great part of *Descriptive Sketches*. Wordsworth was two years distant from his object; but he did not yet understand, I would suppose, the conditions of his art. I will try and show how this was so; and when I have done so, I will point a contrast by calling attention to two passages in the sixth book of the *Prelude* which exhibit, as I think, a remarkable truth to impressions fourteen years old.

Readers of *Descriptive Sketches* have observed with some perplexity that, on the face of it, the poem depicts, not, as it should, a holiday tour, but the objectless wandering of a soul in despair. This is the record, not of an undergraduate tramp, but of the pilgrimage of some *Childe Harold* born out of due time—and very raw in his trade. The poet plainly sets out the cause of his travels at lines 45-6:

Me lured by hope her sorrows to remove
A heart that could not much itself approve.

These lines (of which the grammatical topsy-turveydom may be supposed to mirror a psychical condition) Mr. Harper explains by supposing that Wordsworth was uneasy at offending his relations by going abroad in a Long Vacation which should have been devoted to home study. Yet it is not very plausible that Wordsworth should say—for that is what Mr. Harper makes him say—that his reason for going abroad is that his conscience pricks him for not staying at home. Elsewhere (676) he speaks of his heart as being

> Without one hope her written griefs to blot

save in the grave. It is to be feared that few of us look back with regret so tragically poignant upon a wasted vacation. Again, as he wanders through the villages, the 'maidens eye him with enquiring glance', and detect in his appearance 'crazing care' or 'desperate love'; while Nature, with a discernment drawn, perhaps, from a source not deeper than convention, showers

> Soft on his wounded heart her healing power.

This is indeed an undergraduate taking himself seriously!

It is fortunate (or unfortunate) that Wordsworth has himself left us a contemporary prose account of this Swiss tour, in the form of a letter to his sister. There this lost soul gives the following report of himself:

'I am in excellent health and spirits . . . my spirits have been kept in a perpetual hurry of delight. . . . I feel a high enjoyment in reflecting that perhaps scarcely a day of my life [1] will pass in which I shall not derive . . . happiness from these images . . .'—

and a good deal more in the same buoyant strain.[2] With this letter may be compared *Prelude*, vi. 754:

> A glorious time, a happy time that was!

M. Legouis, more plausible, I think, than Mr. Harper, supposes that the gloomy strain which runs through

---

[1] It may be noticed that, poorly as the results of the Swiss tour figure in *Descriptive Sketches*, Wordsworth did, none the less, long look back to it as a period of genuine spiritual illumination. In the eleventh book of the *Prelude*, among the chief calamities which oppress his mind when he thinks of Napoleon, he reckons the fact that the Alps must now lose for him their old beauty (xi. 409 sqq.).

[2] Harper, i, pp. 93-4.

the poem (and of which he supplies additional illustrations) is a mere modish affectation. Melancholy was a fashionable pose of the time; and in its weeds, M. Legouis thinks, Wordsworth dresses up 'the first vague unrest of his sense and feelings'. There are touches of wistful melancholy in the earlier *Evening Walk*. This explanation perhaps derives some countenance from Wordsworth himself, who, speaking of the tour in *Prelude*, vi, says that he found it sweet

> To feed a poet's tender melancholy
> And fond conceit of sadness.   (vi. 366-7.)

But I think that neither M. Legouis nor Wordsworth himself quite avail to explain away the Byronic gloom of the poem. It is not a mere 'tender melancholy'; it is not in the same order as the fashionable Welt-Schmerz reflected in *An Evening Walk*. It has its source, not in any modish brooding over the pain of the world, but, admittedly, in a strong disapproval of self. Even M. Legouis is forced, before he has finished, to admit that it is no ordinary melancholy. 'Indeed, it is despair', he says, quite plainly.[1]

The simplest explanation, as it seems to me, is to suppose that Wordsworth has infused into the poem some element of the emotions of the period in which it was actually composed: that it reflects—in a confused and unreal fashion—both the first shock of the French Revolution and the episode of Annette; and that the unreality of it arises not from the fact that the poet is describing feelings two years old, but from the fact that he is struggling, in part at any rate, with recent, indeed present, emotions. In the last paragraphs of the poem the scene is actually placed on the banks

[1] *Eng. Trans.*, p. 157.

of the Loire ; Wordsworth, that is to say, takes himself and Jones to a region not in fact visited by them in 1790.[1] But it was here that the poem was written in 1792. The region is apostrophized thus, in lines 739 sqq. :

> And thou, fair favoured region which my soul
> Shall love till life has broke her golden bowl,
> Till death's cold hand her cistern-wheel assail,
> And vain regret and vain desire shall fail.

M. Legouis supposes the region addressed to be France in general, and the passion of the address to be the revolutionary passion. But the context does not justify this wider attribution, and Wordsworth has himself told us that in 1790 he cared very little for the issues of the Revolution. The lines, to my mind, have the note of a very personal sentiment ; and once again I am inclined to think of Annette. I would call attention in this connexion to a number of passages in the poem which are marked by a purely sensuous quality, to which elsewhere in Wordsworth it would be hard to find analogues. We are carried repeatedly into an atmosphere which pervades no other part of Wordsworth : a world of 'dark-eyed maidens', of 'soft bosoms breathing round contagious sighs', of eyes that 'throw the sultry light of young desire', of 'the low-warbled breath of twilight lute'—and of much other rubbish of a like kind (14, 113, 148, 190, 748).

Another element of perplexity is created by occasional hints which the poem furnishes of religious scepticism. ' I think it has never been remarked ', says Mr. Harper, ' that the poem contains a distinct confession of religious

[1] Though Jones was not with Wordsworth on the Loire in 1790, Wordsworth was expecting him there in 1792, when the poem was being finished. The last four lines of the poem, therefore, will be less unreal than, prima facie, they appear.

unbelief. Yet this is plainly the meaning of the four lines which conclude the passage describing the pilgrimage to the shrine of Einsiedeln (676 sqq.). Addressing the credulous worshippers, he cries:

> Without one hope her written griefs to blot
> Save in the land where all things are forgot,
> My heart, alive to transports long unknown,
> Half wishes your delusion were her own.'

Wordsworth suppressed this passage in later editions; and that this mood of religious unbelief did not belong to the Wordsworth of the actual Swiss tour, we may satisfy ourselves by a single passage from the letter to his sister from which I have already quoted. 'Among the awful scenes of the Alps', he writes, 'I had not a thought of man, or of a single created being: my whole soul was turned to him who produced the terrible majesty before me.' *That* was the Wordsworth of 1790; but not of 1792; and it is worth noticing that this conception of a God who makes, rather than is, Nature, hardly recurs in Wordsworth until the *Excursion*. Only there, after twenty years, does Wordsworth get back to what Coleridge called his 'I and my brother the Dean' manner. As to his religious beliefs in 1792-3 we have the testimony, not, I fancy, completely candid, of his nephew the bishop: 'His mind was whirled round in a vortex of doubt.' The reference is to the period immediately following the return from France. 'Not that he ever lapsed into scepticism', the bishop adds.[1] The thought in the *addendum* is, pretty obviously, born of the wish. The biographer is himself aware that, in poems not far removed in date from 1792-3, Wordsworth appears in some danger of 'divinizing the creation

---

[1] *Memoirs*, i, p. 74.

and dishonouring the creator ', and that what he wrote might 'be perverted to a popular and pantheizing philosophy '.[1] After all, it was in 1796 that Coleridge spoke of Wordsworth as still ' at least a semi-atheist '.[2]

In this connexion it is interesting to compare that passage in *Descriptive Sketches* which deals with Wordsworth's visit to the Grande Chartreuse with the lines in the sixth book of the *Prelude* which describe the same incident. Wordsworth found the Chartreuse in possession of the revolutionary soldiery. In *Descriptive Sketches* the incident is viewed in a manner somewhat obviously detached and sceptical. Though he talks of 'Blasphemy within the shuddering fane', yet it is not difficult to see that, upon the whole, he derives some satisfaction from the fact that ' the power whose frown severe ' used to ' tame reason till she crouched in fear ' (i.e. the power of religious superstition) is now obliged to crouch before the revolutionary arms of ' Reason '. But the mood was not that of 1790. The mood of 1790 is more faithfully preserved in the *Prelude*. There Wordsworth describes the acute conflict set up in his mind between his ardour for revolutionary freedom and his sense of religion ; and the passage ends in a prayer for ' these courts of mystery ', this place of ' penitential tears and trembling hopes ', which he treads ' in sympathetic reverence '.[3]

This is one of the two passages in the sixth book to which I promised to call attention, as illustrating the greater veracity and depth of the account of the Swiss tour given in the *Prelude*. The other, rather different in kind, is the well-known passage describing the crossing

[1] *Ib.*, pp. 117–18.   [2] *Letters*, i, p. 164. See also *ib.*, p. 246.
[3] *Descr. Sk.*, 53 sqq. ; *Prelude*, vi, 414 sqq.

of the Alps.[1] It is the central episode of the whole
tour, as depicted in the *Prelude*, the one great and deep
memory. Crossing the Simplon Pass, Wordsworth and
his friend became, for a space, parted from their guide.
They proceeded to climb, in the belief that their way
still led upward, nearer and nearer to the clouds. While
they were expecting still to rise, they met a peasant,
of whom they inquired the way, and who informed them
that their proper route was in fact downward. Without
knowing it they had crossed the Alps. The disillusion-
ment was at the moment baffling; and here is Wordsworth's account of it. Imagination, he says, that
'awful power',

> rose from the mind's abyss
> Like an unfathered vapour that enwraps,
> At once, some lonely traveller. I was lost;
> Halted without an effort to break through;
> But to my conscious soul I *now* can say—
> 'I recognize thy glory'; in such strength
> Of usurpation, when the light of sense
> Goes out, but with a flush that has revealed
> The invisible world, doth greatness make abode,
> There harbours; whether we be young or old,
> Our destiny, our being's heart and home,
> Is with infinitude, and only there,
> With hope it is, hope that can never die,
> Effort and expectation and desire,
> And something evermore about to be.

Here it is to be noted, firstly that this central and
supreme memory of the tour is lost wholly from *Descriptive Sketches*—not a word of it will you find there; and
secondly, that what may be called the good faith of
this memory is amply attested by the careful distinction
which Wordsworth makes between his later, and his

[1] *Prelude*, vi. 562 sqq.

original, perception. At the actual time of the experience, the imaginative power was like a wet mist, shrouding his faculties, in which he was halted and lost. It was many years later that he 'recognized the glory'. While he held always to the doctrine that the truth of nature is given to us by the senses, he failed, in his early contacts with the external world, to 'recognize' the manner in which this in fact takes place; it was only later that he became aware of what is ultimately a fundamental truth for him, namely, that our highest perceptions come to us, through sense, indeed, but in and by the extinction of sense—when sense, in the act of being extinguished, throws a light upon the world beyond sense.[1]

The concluding portion of *Descriptive Sketches* contains political reflections which are obviously, and, I think, admittedly, coloured by the events of 1791–2.[2] These political reflections are in the main remarkable only for the fact that they are expressed in a manner the most artificial conceivable, the most unreal. I will notice only two matters of detail.

In line 706 Savoy is apostrophized as the 'slave of slaves'. A foot-note informs us that the passage was written before 'the emancipation of Savoy', though the poet regards it as 'scarce necessary' to point this out (to readers at once intelligent and sympathetic). Here we have the revolutionary with a vengeance. The annexation of Savoy by France is accepted as, on the

[1] For this distinction between immediate perception and subsequent ideal recognition, cf. *Prelude*, vi, p. 739, where Wordsworth emphasizes the fact that many of the impressions of the tour were not instantaneous in their effects, but led only in a devious fashion to effects perceived long afterwards.

[2] Lines 787–91 reflect, I would suggest, the episode (1792) related in *Prelude*, ix. 509–18.

face of it, her 'emancipation'. As good a comment upon the passage as any other is furnished by Burns. Burns 'commenced revolutionary' in as fine a spirit as Wordsworth. 'As for France', he says, 'I was her enthusiastic votary at the beginning of the business.' 'But when', he adds, 'she came to show her old avidity for conquest in annexing Savoy, &c., to her dominions, and invading the rights of Holland, I altered my sentiments.' Burns is thinking, as the reference to Holland shows, of a date somewhat later. But it is worth while, when the influence of the French Revolution upon British poetry is spoken of, to bring these two passages together.

Lines 780 sqq. show Wordsworth prepared for a new heaven and a new earth, which are perhaps to be won only by 'rousing hell's own aid'.[1] The effect of the struggle for freedom may be, he says, to set the world in flames. Yet from the 'innocuous flames'—they became a good deal less innocuous later—there will come a 'lovely birth':

> Nature, as in her prime, her virgin reign
> Begins, and Love and Truth compose her train.

The sense given here to the word 'Nature' is derived obviously from the system of Rousseau, the spiritual father of the Revolution. The French Revolution is as yet for Wordsworth the 'return to Nature' in its most naïve signification (not infrequently elsewhere the word 'Nature' is given the same meaning, e.g. *Prelude*, xi. 31 [2]). Wordsworth suppressed the lines in the later

[1] 781: the crudity of the phrase (reminiscent, perhaps, of Virgil's *flectere si nequeo superos Acheronta movebo*) is noteworthy. See Coleridge: *Ode to the Departing Year*, 31–3.

[2] In reading Wordsworth, it is always worth stopping to ask oneself, in any given passage, in what sense he is using the word

edition of the poem; and a significant comment upon them (and upon their suppression) is furnished by the language of the disillusioned revolutionary in the third book of the *Excursion*:

> Nature was my guide,
> The nature of the dissolute. (*Exc.* iii. 807.)

The source of Wordsworth's artificial manner in *Descriptive Sketches* has been correctly indicated by M. Legouis. Wordsworth's poetic theory and practice in this period are derived from Erasmus Darwin, the grandfather of the great naturalist, and the author of a didactic poem, *The Botanical Garden*. Nobody now reads *The Botanical Garden*; yet at one time its author was thought by Coleridge to be ' the first literary figure in Europe '.[1] The different parts of the poem are interlarded with dialogues, in prose, upon the theory of poetry and art. ' The Muses are young ladies ', says Darwin, ' and we expect to see them dressed.' And dressed they are, both in the *Botanical Garden* and in *Descriptive Sketches*; and their taste in dress is very bad indeed. But Darwin was not only a poet, with a theory of poetic diction; what is for our purpose, I fancy, much more important—and what M. Legouis omits to tell us—is

nature. *Prelude*, xi. 31 illustrates this well. Even where he uses ' nature ' as the equivalent of the external world, or our experience of it, it is his habit to colour that meaning with meanings derived from many of the other very vague uses of the word. ' Nature ' stands often as the equivalent of the elementary principle of un-intellectualized goodness in the world of both men and things: the antithesis of custom and formal reason. The different shades of meaning given to the word in the Revolutionary poets generally would furnish the theme of an interesting essay.

[1] Hazlitt remarks that ' Coleridge always somehow contrived to prefer the unknown to the known ' (*My First Acquaintance with Poets*). But the vogue of Darwin was undoubtedly considerable, especially in the ranks of the free-thinkers.

that he was, in religion, a prominent free-thinker, and, in politics, an advanced radical. He was personally acquainted with, and carried on correspondence with, Rousseau. I know no evidence of any personal relations between Darwin and Wordsworth. But Darwin was an old member of Wordsworth's own college, St. John's; and from Christopher Wordsworth's *English Universities in the Eighteenth Century* we know that Darwin read, and admired, *Descriptive Sketches* on its first appearance. It is, I think, more than likely that, if only indirectly, he was in part responsible for the revolutionary and free-thinking turn given to Wordsworth's mind in 1791 and the following years.

Before I leave *Descriptive Sketches* I may mention a phenomenon in connexion with them which illustrates their unreality in a manner rather surprising—I owe the notice of it, once again, to M. Legouis. In notes to lines 372 and 475 Wordsworth mentions his indebtedness to the French poet and naturalist, Ramond de Carbonnières. M. Legouis has shown that his debt to this writer extends far beyond the two passages in which it is acknowledged. Wordsworth not only sees objects at second-hand, through the medium of Ramond's notes, but he sometimes puts this writer's ideas into his verses 'even where those ideas are at variance with his own impressions'. Examples of this are collected by M. Legouis, to whose book I may refer the reader.

iii

GODWIN AND GODWINISM

WORDSWORTH left France, pretty certainly, in December 1792;[1] and in February of the following year were published both *An Evening Walk* and *Descriptive Sketches*. It is perhaps worth noting that the publisher was Joseph Johnson of St. Paul's Churchyard—Johnson's press was a good deal employed by the heretics of the time, political and religious. He was himself a friend of the arch-heretic, William Godwin; and he published for Priestley and Horne Tooke and Gilbert Wakefield (the publication of a pamphlet of Wakefield led, in 1797, to his prosecution), as well as for Erasmus Darwin (*The Botanical Garden* was Johnson's undertaking).

Godwin's *Political Justice* was published in the same month; and it was in this month also that war was declared between England and revolutionary France. These two events are of first-rate importance for Wordsworth's development, and their interconnexion requires explanation and emphasis.

When Wordsworth passed through France in 1790, on his way to Switzerland, his interest in the Revolution (the tide of which Mirabeau was then endeavouring to arrest) was no greater, it was perhaps less, than that of

[1] Wordsworth, in the 1850 version of the *Prelude*, speaks of himself as returning to England ' dragged by a chain of harsh necessity '. This is commonly interpreted as a periphrasis for want of money. The interpretation is confirmed by the earliest version of the *Prelude* which speaks of ' absolute want Of Funds for my support '.

any other Englishman who talked the ordinary English cant of Liberty. We know this from himself.

> Nature then was sovereign in my mind,

he says. Man, and his affairs, took a second place—
' his hour being not yet come '.[1] In 1790

> France standing on the top of golden hours
> And human nature seeming born again

made only such appeal to him as it necessarily must to a mind romantic and adventurous; an appeal which was casual, and secondary wholly to the appeal of the Alps, of Nature. The ' hour of Man ' was later; and its coming can be dated with some precision. It is, indeed, dated by Wordsworth himself with characteristic exactness. ' Until not less Than two-and-twenty summers had been told Was man in my affections and regard Subordinate ', he tells us plainly, in the eighth book of the *Prelude*.[2] Plainly; but apparently not plainly enough for his editors; since even Mr. Hutchinson conceives the reference here to be to the year 1792. But Wordsworth was born in April; and when he reckons by seasons, he is always meticulously accurate. The reference is, clearly, to the year 1791; and the point is of some importance: since it means that the interest in Man was not first acquired in France, as is commonly supposed, and under the influence of Beaupuy; but that it was this interest which, acquired in England, took him to France for the second time in 1792. Beaupuy was a revolutionary captain, later a general, with whom Wordsworth formed, in 1792-3, a close friendship, and who undoubtedly did much to clarify and deepen his political reflection. The effects

---

[1] *Prelude*, vi. 333 sqq.: viii. 340-56. [2] 349-51.

upon Wordsworth's mind of the influence of Beaupuy, and of the course of the Revolution during his sojourn in France, can hardly perhaps be exaggerated. But they can easily be, at certain points, misconceived; and I fancy that this not uncommonly happens.

Wordsworth himself is our best guide, and in following him we are wise if we emphasize what he emphasizes. He lays a somewhat special emphasis upon the fact that his experience of the Revolution did not come upon him as a storm in any sort. Criticism has been so long obsessed by the false image of a mild and home-keeping Wordsworth that it is still not a little difficult for us to realize that to himself at least Wordsworth appeared a man made for the Revolution—and it for him. Not only was it not an experience which overwhelmed him, subverting (as we are apt to conceive) the whole fabric of his habitual life, but it scarcely availed to startle him. In the *Prelude* he is most careful to explain to us that the Revolution presented itself to his thinking and feeling as *the most natural thing in the world*. At first, indeed, it found him almost indifferent:

> I stood 'mid these concussions unconcerned
> —Tranquil almost.

There are other conjunctures where, to understand him, we have to reckon with this odd *sang froid* in him. The source of it, in 1791–2, he traces for us. He conceives that throughout his life (till the end of 1792) the whole trend of his mind has been *in the direction of nature and freedom*; and just upon this account, the events of the Revolution, as he beheld them developing in France, so far from shaking mind or habit in him,

> Seemed nothing out of Nature's certain course.

but,
> A gift that was come rather late than soon.
> (ix. 247–8.)

It is important to bear this in mind because, only so far as we do so, shall we be able to appraise the effects upon him of the month of February 1793. Until the moment when, in that month, France declared war upon England, Wordsworth regards his life as having been one continuous process of natural development. His words, in this connexion, are memorable:

> No shock
> Given to my moral nature had I known
> Down to that very moment: neither lapse
> Nor turn of sentiment that might be named
> A revolution,[1] save at this one time;
> All else was progress on the self-same path
> On which, with a diversity of pace,
> I had been travelling.

Now the flow of his whole nature towards freedom seemed suddenly blocked by the declaration of war. To understand his situation clearly we must bear in mind that he was still under the influence of Rousseau. This meant two things. First: in respect of the individual, the essential condition of the good life was a free development towards nature. Secondly: in respect of society, the condition of the good lay in the self-expression of the general will; and in the French Revolution Wordsworth had seemed to himself to hear the first stammerings of this self-expression.

Now, so far as he himself was concerned, the free movement towards Nature was suddenly disturbed. His moral being became torn by the conflicting claims of

---
[1] Clearly the word is not used here by accident.

country and the world. The City of Cecrops was ranged against the City of Zeus. Very soon the trouble was to be deepened by the discovery that the Revolution, instead of realizing an ideal society in which the general will was going to become harmoniously articulate, was moving rapidly in a direction inimical to all freedom; and was not only crushing the individual, but seemed intent to afford proof that the nature of the individual was incapable of realization under *any* form of human society or government: seemed intent, in fact, on proving the main thesis of Godwinism.

I propose, with the aid of the *Prelude*, to try and follow the process by which Wordsworth went over to Godwinism; to mark the effects of Godwinism in the poetry of his Godwinian period; and, finally, to consider the nature of the means by which he saved himself out of Godwinism, and settled into the strength of his great decade.[1]

The problem is a good deal complicated by the circumstance that it is, to my mind, certain that, as Wordsworth originally sketched this part of the *Prelude*, he had intended either to omit altogether, or to treat very cursorily, his period of discipleship to Godwin. This is, I believe, the only possible explanation of the form of the poem as it lies before us in Books X and XI. To make

[1] I have deliberately left upon one side the detail of Wordsworth's sojourn in France. In doing so I have been guided, in the main, by the considerations already adduced—Wordsworth's real moral crisis belongs to 1793, not to 1791-2. I have also been unwilling, in connexion with the Annette episode, I will not say to pry, but to pry to no purpose. In respect of this episode it is not hard to show perspicacity, and it is easy to lose perspective. I have, however, appended to this Section a foot-note in which I have offered upon the subject of the French sojourn, some remarks which, while they sufficiently mark my sense of a lacuna, may, I hope, be regarded as not violating the rules, if there be any, of taste and proportion.

this clear, it is necessary to consider the text for a few moments in rather tedious detail.

At x. 236 Wordsworth takes up his story from the time of his return to England in December 1792 (the declaration of war is mentioned at 263 sqq.). The end of the book brings us down to the death of Robespierre. The first 73 lines of Book XI deal with the milder period in France immediately succeeding the Terror; and with the repressive policy pursued in England by Pitt, in domestic affairs. Then suddenly at line 74 Wordsworth proceeds to summarize the account already given in Book IX of his early contact with the Revolution. At line 173 he returns to the declaration of war in February 1793; and at 194 begins the history of his movement towards Godwinism. This occupies lines 194–320; and at 321 he begins to narrate how he was led, first from Godwin to Spinozism, and then gradually (very largely under the influence of his sister Dorothy) back to Nature. The theme of this conversion is continued in Book XII, where, however, the main thread is somewhat broken at 44–207 by a partial further exposition of the effects of Godwinism, and by an explanation of the manner in which it corrupted the poet's perception of Nature.

There is obviously here an odd duplication in the narrative—which comes back at xi. 173 to the point reached at x. 263, and inserts in the latter passage, as a kind of afterthought, the very interesting account of Godwinism which had been omitted from the former book. It is difficult to resist the suspicion that the original omission was deliberate. When it was made, Wordsworth had intended to keep Godwin out of the picture. Subsequently that instinct for truthfulness, which is paramount with him, compelled him to recast his plan.

Godwin and Godwinism

Throughout the *Prelude* Godwin is nowhere mentioned by name; and it is in that part of the *Prelude* which speaks of him that Wordsworth warns us—as I have already noticed—that he considers himself obliged to exercise a certain reserve (xi. 284 sqq.). Whether this reserve is on his own account, or Godwin's, or for the sake of youthful disciples, is not determined; but those who know Wordsworth best will be inclined to think that the last consideration alone weighed with him. To what extent Wordsworth was personally acquainted with Godwin, is uncertain. A letter that he wrote to Godwin in 1811 does not decide the question: in it, characteristically, he asks Godwin not to send him presents of books upon which he has to pay 4s. 6d. postage.[1] Whether one writes thus to one's personal friends depends perhaps on the degree both of intimacy and of provocation. For myself, I should be inclined to infer from the letter that Godwin had at an earlier date been personally known to Wordsworth; but that Wordsworth, in what is at best a rude letter, would like him to understand that the acquaintance was of the slightest.[2] There is, however, no doubt either of the Godwinism of Wordsworth, or that these passages of the *Prelude* speak of Godwin and no one else.

To-day no one reads Godwin, neither his *Political Justice* nor his novels. Yet, of the novels, *Caleb Williams* at least is still readable, and is accessible in a cheap reprint. It was accounted in its time an immortal book; and, as will appear presently, it exercised a powerful influence upon Wordsworth. Of the system outlined

[1] *Letters of the Wordsworth Family*, i, p. 515.
[2] Some degree of acquaintance is attested by Crabb Robinson, *Diary*, ii, p. 7.

in *Political Justice* some account is necessary; for with the understanding of it is involved the understanding of an important part, not only of Wordsworth, but of Coleridge, of Southey, of Shelley. It is not easy to-day to recapture the conditions of Godwin's far-felt and deeply felt influence. It belongs to a mode of life and thought, and to a political and social environment, of which there can find their way to us only thin airs and fluitant echoes. Perhaps Hazlitt's essay, ' Mr. Godwin ', in the *Spirit of the Age*, is still more helpful than anything else—indeed, in the *Spirit of the Age*, as a whole, the casual student has a better chance than elsewhere of seizing the spirit, or one part of it, of the age of Wordsworth. This may serve, perhaps, as an apology for appending here an extract from Hazlitt of a length somewhat disproportionate. Certainly Hazlitt never wrote in a style more lively and telling, nor upon a theme more congenial, than when he wrote of Godwin : [1]

' The Spirit of the Age ', writes Hazlitt in 1825, ' was never more fully shewn than in its treatment of this writer—its love of paradox and change, its dastard submission to prejudice and to the fashion of the day. Five and twenty years ago he was in the very zenith of a sultry and unwholesome popularity. He blazed as a sun in the firmament of reputation. No one was more talked of, more looked up to, more sought after; and wherever liberty, truth, justice was the theme, his name was not far off. Now he has sunk below the horizon, and enjoys the serene twilight of a doubtful immortality. Mr. Godwin, during his life-time, has secured to himself the triumphs and the mortifications of an extreme notoriety and of a sort of posthumous fame. His bark,

[1] The essay in the *Spirit of the Age* may profitably be supplemented by the same writer's critique in the *Edinburgh Review* for April 1830 (Waller-Glover, x, pp. 385 sqq.).

after being tossed in the revolutionary tempest, now raised to heaven by all the fury of popular breath, now almost dashed in pieces, and buried in the quicksands of ignorance, or scorched with the lightning of momentary indignation, at length floats on the calm wave that is to bear it down the stream of time. Mr. Godwin's person is not known, he is not pointed out in the street, his conversation is not courted, his opinions are not asked, he is at the head of no cabal, he belongs to no party in the state, he has no train of admirers, no one thinks it worth while even to traduce and vilify him, he has scarcely friend or foe; the world makes a point (as Goldsmith used to say) of taking no more notice of him than if such an individual had never existed. He is to all ordinary intents and purposes dead and buried. But the author of *Political Justice* and of *Caleb Williams* can never die. His name is an abstraction in letters, his works are standard in the history of intellect. He is thought of now like any eminent writer of 150 years ago, or just as he will be 150 years hence. He knows this, and smiles in silent mockery of himself, reposing on the monument of his fame—

sedet aeternumque sedebit infelix.

' No work in our time gave such a blow to the philosophical mind of the country as the celebrated *Enquiry concerning Political Justice*. Tom Paine was for the time as a Tom Fool to him, Paley an old woman, Edmund Burke a flashy sophist. Truth, moral truth, it was supposed, had here taken up its abode; and these were the oracles of thought. " Throw aside your books of chemistry ", said Wordsworth to a young man, a student of the Temple, " and read Godwin upon Necessity." Sad necessity. Fatal reverse! Is truth then so variable? Is it one thing at twenty and another at forty? Is it a burning heat in 1793, and below zero in 1814? Not so, in the name of manhood and common sense! Let us pause here a little. Mr. Godwin indulged in extreme opinions, and carried with him all the most sanguine and fearless minds of the time. What then? Because these opinions were overcharged, were they therefore altogether groundless? Is the very god of our idolatry all of a sudden become an abomination and an anathema? Could so many young men of talent, of education, and of principle have been hurried away by what had neither truth nor nature, not one particle of honest feeling, nor the least show of reason in it? Is the Modern Philosophy, as it has been called, at one moment a youthful bride, and the next a withered beldame, like the false Duessa in Spenser? Or is the vaunted edifice of Reason, like his House of Pride, gorgeous in front, and dazzling to approach, while " its hinder parts are ruinous, decayed, and old "? Has the main prop, which supported the mighty fabric, been shaken and given way under the strong grasp of some Samson? or has it not rather been undermined by rats and vermin? At one time it almost seemed that " if this failed

> The pillared firmament was rottenness,
> And earth's base built of stubble ";

now scarce a shadow of it remains, it is crumbled to dust nor is it ever talked of! What then went ye forth to see, a reed shaken by the wind? Was it for this that our young gownsmen of the highest education and promise, versed in classic lore, steeped in dialectics, armed at all points for the foe, well read, well nurtured, well provided for, left the university and the prospect of lawn sleeves, tearing asunder the shackles of the freeborn spirit and the cobwebs of school-divinity, to throw themselves at the feet of the new Gamaliel, and learn wisdom from him? Was it for this that students at the bar, acute, inquisitive, sceptical (here only wild enthusiasts), neglected for a while the paths of preferment and the law as too narrow, tortuous, and unseemly to bear the pure and broad light of reason? Was it for this that students in medicine missed their way to lectureships and the top of their professions, deeming lightly of the health of the body and dreaming only of

the renovation of society and the march of the human
mind? Was it to this that Mr. Southey's *Inscriptions*
pointed, to this that Mr. Coleridge's *Religious Musings*
tended? Was it for this that Mr. Godwin himself sat
with arms folded and "like Cato gave his little senate
laws"? Or rather, like another Prospero, uttered syl-
lables that with their enchanted breath were to change
the world and might almost stop the stars in their
courses? Oh, and is all forgot? Is the sun of intellect
blotted from the sky? Or has it suffered total eclipse?
Or is it we who make the fancied gloom, by looking at
it through the paltry broken stained fragments of our
own interests and prejudices? Were we fools then, or
are we dishonest now? Or was the impulse of the mind
less likely to be true and sound when it arose from high
thought and pure feeling than afterwards when it was
warped and debased by the example, the vices, and
follies of the world? . . . Mr. Godwin . . . conceived too
nobly of his fellows!'

I have set out this elaborate panegyric, not because
I think it is true, but to illustrate the temper of the
times, and in fairness to Godwin—and to Wordsworth. If I were to speak my own mind, I should be inclined to say of Godwin what Nietzsche said of Wagner,
that he was 'not a man but a disease'. Godwin is a
disease of English poetry for thirty years; from 1793,
when *Political Justice* appeared, until 1822, the year
which saw the death of Godwin's last, and in some
ways most distinguished victim, his son-in-law, Shelley.
Shelley somewhere or other tells us that over a long
period he never went to sleep without reading a page
of *Political Justice*. My own experience, I feel moved
to confess, is the inverse. Over a period, if not long,
at any rate tedious, I have never been able to read
a page of *Political Justice* without going to sleep. Nor,
I may say plainly and at once, have I ever been able to

discover in it anything more noteworthy than the ordinary nonsense of English individualism—carried, however, to a point where it is saved from being silly by becoming definitely insane. And it is perhaps worth while, in connexion with the general movement which Godwin represents, to notice an important distinction between English and French liberalism. This distinction consists in the fact that, while in France the extreme left wing of liberalism is commonly in times of crisis led by a man of genius, in England it is nearly always led by a crank. Godwin never crosses the thin, but clearly marked, line which separates the crank from the man of genius.

Be that as it may, we have to recognize, however reluctantly, that the study of English poetry of the end of the eighteenth and beginning of the nineteenth century is only intelligible in the light of English political theory. That is something that cannot be too often said; and it is because of this that it is worth while to try to understand Godwinism, and the relation of Godwinism to the teaching of Rousseau.

In the preface to the first edition of *Political Justice*, Godwin acknowledges his indebtedness to three philosophical writers: Holbach, Helvetius, Rousseau; and it may be thought doubtful whether he develops any ideas which are not perversions of the ideas of one or other of these three. From Holbach he took, and developed, the view that Reason, which is merely physical science applied to the behaviour of Man in society, teaches us that Man can be happy only by making others happy. From Helvetius he took the opinion that intellect and virtue are conditioned at all points by the form of government under which men live: this is a more overpowering influence than any other: indeed, since it is government which determines education, it is an influence to which it is difficult to assign any limits. In respect of Rousseau his position is not so simple. It is to some extent indicated by a passage in volume ii of *Political Justice* (p. 125, ed. 2), where Rousseau's *Emile* is praised and his *Social Contract* disparaged. The motive of this discrimination is not hard to discover. Between these two works of Rousseau there is an admitted contradiction. The gospel of *Emile* is individual self-development, in accordance with Nature. The gospel of the *Social Contract* is the establishment of the general will, and the merging in that of the individual will. To Godwin, as I have already said, the general will is merely a new form of tyranny. To him, as to Paine, the author of the *Rights of Man*, ' society is produced by our wants, and government by our wickedness ' (i, p. 84).

The *Social Contract*, therefore, is necessarily anathema to Godwin : so indeed is all contract. Contract, believed by so many to be the foundation of morality, is to Godwin in itself immoral. To make any kind of contract is to mortgage our future liberty of reasonable action. To the good man, any treaty is a scrap of paper. And even *Emile*, welcome to Godwin for its assertion of individualism, is really, from any other point of view, equally anathema to him. Its cardinal conception is the return to Nature. But for Nature Godwin has no use. He has no interest in anything less lofty than Reason. There is no law save that of Reason. Many philosophers had said that. Godwin goes a step further, and lays it down that there is no valid reason save that of the individual. Collective Reason is only another name for a general will, a tyranny.

The system of Godwin, then, marks a reaction against Rousseau—and against the conception of the French

Revolution; and it is not difficult to see how it made its immense appeal exactly at this conjuncture, and precisely to that class of mind which it affected most deeply. *Political Justice* coincided with the declaration of war—an event which, erecting for Wordsworth and Coleridge and their friends a barrier between themselves and their country, seemed to point the hopelessness of attempting to reconcile the moral claims of the individual with those of any form of government; and its influence was before long enhanced by the impression of the Terror in France, and by the criminal aggression of French imperialism. Godwin is usually styled a philosophic anarchist. Yet to himself and his first disciples, not only was his system not anarchic, it was essentially a protest against anarchy. To Godwin society is the Great Anarch. Society is, indeed, the one and only source of anarchy; and the only sure refuge from anarchy is the individual reason. On the text 'Society the Great Anarch' the French Revolution became, as it developed, a powerful, and, as it might almost seem, convincing commentary. Hence it is that from the month of February 1793, onwards, Godwin lies like a shadow across the whole of English poetry.

NOTE

Wordsworth went to France in 1791 with a disposition prepared for what he found: a temperament formed to regard the Revolution as *the most natural thing in the world*. And he watched the storm at first with something like unconcern. He took with him, however, to France an inadequate knowledge both of history and of the philosophy of history. It was this lack, I should suppose, that Beaupuy supplied. At least it is this part of his influence which Wordsworth emphasizes (see especially *Prelude* ix. 322–39). Nothing in the narrative suggests a proselytising ardour of revolution in Beaupuy, or any sort of ' conversion ' in Wordsworth. The influence should be thought of as mainly regulative. Wordsworth was not without a certain northern canniness, which made him able to look after himself.

There is another aspect of Beaupuy to which Wordsworth directs attention—a certain ' passion and gallantry '; which ' in his idler day ' he ' had paid to woman ' (ix. 311–13). It was, moreover, from Beaupuy that Wordsworth, according to his own account (and that this is probably an error of memory does not much matter), first learned the story of Vaudracour and Julia. It has been supposed that this story, as Wordsworth tells it, reflects in some degree the Annette episode (the suggestion was made by Mr. Harper). Another French officer, unnamed, belonging to the royalist faction, with whom Wordsworth became associated, is described as one who, earlier, ' had sate lord in many tender hearts ' (ix. 139 sqq.). These references sufficiently indicate, I think, that, during his French sojourn, Wordsworth, a youth fresh from college, newly dipped in a philosophy which tended to glorify the natural instincts of man, was brought somewhat suddenly into a society of a kind hitherto unfamiliar to him: a society of which the conventions were, in important particulars, different from those of which he had experience. This is no doubt what is meant to be expressed by some guarded sentences of his first biographer. ' Wordsworth's condition in France ', says Bishop Wordsworth, ' was a very critical one . . . he was encompassed by strong temptations.' He was in fact thrown into an environment where ' passion and gallantry ' were the unregulated prerogative of youth, where, to use a striking phrase of Tacitus, *corrumpere et corrumpi saeculum vocabatur*. Whether Wordsworth himself at the time regarded the Annette episode with the seriousness with which he, without doubt, viewed it at a later date, we have no means of knowing. He made no attempt at the time to regularize the connexion; and the reasons offered by Mr. Harper (in *Wordsworth's French Daughter*) for his not marrying

Annette do not appear to me particularly cogent. Nothing in his writings suggests that among the troubles of his conscience, in the period following his return to England, moral concern (using that phrase in its vulgar and narrow sense) was predominant. At a much later date, it was, in a sense, open to him to marry Annette. But the difficulties and incongruities of such a course, at that later date, were so considerable, and are so obvious, that charity, I think, will be inclined to endorse the decision which common sense then made.

The *Prelude*, of course, contains no hint of the episode. The *Prelude* is, in any case, not a *Confessions*, nor Wordsworth a Rousseau. On the other hand, the more I read the *Prelude*, the more I am disposed to feel that, in it, Wordsworth has tried to put to us those parts of his experience which he believed, in a deep sense, to *matter*. And in general I am inclined to the belief that, not only are poets commonly a more truthful race than other men, but that they frequently understand themselves better than other people understand them. That is why I am inclined to suppose that, to Wordsworth, reviewing the history of his spiritual development, the Annette episode did not present itself as a part of his life in which his passions and feelings had been seriously engaged. It must be added, however, that his habit (which we have already remarked) of seeing certain images of himself and his behaviour as though they were part of another personality is one that might easily breed a detachment from moral responsibilities. It is undoubtedly the source in Wordsworth of a good deal of behaviour strangely deficient in humour. When all is said and done, there is something not a little ludicrous in the month's visit which, in 1820, Wordsworth paid to Paris (in order to be near Annette and his daughter), in the company, not merely of Mrs. Wordsworth, but of Dorothy, Crabb Robinson, Mr. and Mrs. Monkhouse, and Mrs. Horrocks! The mentality of this holiday party is not easily appraised. (See *Wordsworth's French Daughter*, pp. 10–11.)

IV

1793

PRECISELY at what points Wordsworth's Godwinian period begins and ends is a difficult question, upon which we have, for the most part, only such guidance as is afforded by his own writings. To his Godwinian period, however, belong two compositions of first-rate interest: *Guilt and Sorrow*, and the dramatic poem of *The Borderers*. I propose to speak briefly of each of these poems; but, for a proper understanding of them, it is necessary that I should try to reconstitute, with the aid of the *Prelude*, the conditions out of which they arose. I must ask the patience of the reader, therefore, while I try to follow Wordsworth's own narrative, as it is there given, from the point of his return to England in December 1792, down to the point at which he took up the composition of *Guilt and Sorrow*. When I have attempted some characterization of that poem, I shall have to tax yet further the reader's faculty for assimilating dry bones, while I attempt to make intelligible the biographical sequences of the period between *Guilt and Sorrow* and *The Borderers*. One or two preliminary observations, anticipating the conclusions of a rather tiresome discussion, may perhaps be helpful as guiding threads by which the main course of the narrative may be apprehended.

The Godwinian period begins in 1793 and ends some time in 1797. But it has two main divisions. Of these the first, and longest, lies between the spring of 1793 and the summer of 1795; and may be called the epoch of semi-Godwinism. Wordsworth describes himself as having, during this period, 'lent but a careless ear' to the pretensions of Godwin, which were, however, 'sedulously urged' upon him.[1] We shall see reason, I fancy, to think that he considerably under-estimates the degree to which, in these years, he felt the influence of Godwin. The influence was deep, but not sufficiently deep to exclude other influences and hopes—influences and hopes which were, in fact, not logically compatible with it. The period of the fuller Godwinism is dated, so far as its beginning is concerned, with exactness—by Wordsworth himself. It begins in July 1795. It ends, without any time specification, in *Lyrical Ballads:* we pass there, suddenly and surprisedly, into the sunshine— by the kind of miracle which sometimes accomplishes itself for the traveller who travels to Italy by way of the St. Gothard tunnel : he enters it from grey and snow-laden northern skies, and, as his train leaves it twenty minutes later, it unrolls before his unprepared gaze the sun-bathed plains of Lombardy and an anomalous world of exuberant spring. Indeed, it is notable that all Wordsworth's crises fall unawares. Like the visitations of angels and of demons, they happen without the just accumulation of their antecedents. That this is so, we shall see ; and I call it notable, not for the reason that it does not fit with what should be expected of poets, but because it serves to remind us that Wordsworth is, as little as any other poet, exempt from the primal condition of poetry—the winds of impulse blow where they list, and, swifter than a man without poetry can leap a brook, they lift their poet from the one pole of life to the other. Even so, it should be added that before most of Wordsworth's crises there goes a darkness.

[1] See below, p. 88.

Quite apart from the period of his sojourn in France there are two periods in his life, each of them of about six months' duration, in which his doings and thinking are entirely withdrawn from biographical investigation. They are the first half of the year 1793 and the first half, or rather more, of the year 1795. During these two periods, Wordsworth is completely withdrawn from our knowledge; and perhaps in this darkness, at present impenetrable, and not to be penetrated without some degree of superstitious reverence, the pangs were prepared,

> The internal pangs were ready, the dread strife
> Of poor humanity's afflicted will

and of the soul of poetry swept tumultuously to its own unguessed fulfilments.

The narrative which we have to follow begins at line 236 of the tenth book of the *Prelude*. In lines 236–62 Wordsworth tells us that, on his return to England, he went to live in London. He was too deeply absorbed in the interests of the Revolution to have any interest in Nature, or to be able to hide himself in the country. The ' hour of Man ' had come with a vengeance. So great was his absorption in French affairs that even the agitation for the abolition of the slave-trade seemed to him a minor matter. If France prospered, then Liberty of its own strength must assuredly spread to all parts of the world.

Lines 263–83 describe his feelings on the outbreak of war with France. To this I have already referred; and may here be content to reiterate the importance of marking the date February 1793, as that of the first great spiritual crisis in Wordsworth's life. The narrative then carries us—once we catch the skill to follow its oddly devious course—it carries us swiftly to the second crisis. Indeed, too swiftly. At line 284 Wordsworth says that even 'afterwards' he exulted in the news of a British defeat. This 'afterwards' is made more specific in the lines immediately following. The defeat referred to is that sustained in the Battle of Hondschoote, fought in September 1793 (286–7). By that time Wordsworth was no longer in London—for lines 315–30 describe how at Spithead he watched the naval preparations for war. That was in the month of July 1793. In that month, we know from other sources, he went, with his friend William Calvert,[1] to the Isle of Wight. He tells us himself, in the preface to *Guilt and Sorrow*, and again in the Fenwick Notes, that he was in the island a whole month.

At line 330 occurs a break in the narrative; which shifts back suddenly to French affairs. The gap may be filled in from another book of the *Prelude*. In Book xiii Wordsworth refers, without date, to a memorable wandering over Salisbury Plain, during the course of which—he says—there was borne in on him for the first time the belief that he possessed the insight of a poet capable of work 'creative and enduring', with ' a power like Nature's'. Here we may suppose ourselves to reach what I will call the second great crisis of his development; and we can date it fairly exactly. The wandering referred to was a tour, undertaken after leaving the Isle of Wight in August 1793, from Salisbury, over the Plain, through the west of England, and Monmouthshire, along the Wye by Tintern into Wales. The facts, and the date, come to us from Wordsworth himself. Fifty years

[1] Brother of Raisley Calvert, from whom, shortly afterwards, Wordsworth received the legacy to which he owed his independence.

subsequently he said (dictating the Fenwick Notes):
' My ramble over Salisbury Plain, put me . . . upon
writing *Guilt and Sorrow*, and left upon my mind
imaginative impressions the force of which I have felt
to this day.'

To understand the nature of these imaginative impressions, we must go, first, to the passage of *Prelude*
xiii, to which I have just referred, and secondly, to
the poem upon *Tintern Abbey*. In *Prelude* xiii, 367 sqq.,
he says:

                      I remember well
That in life's everyday experiences
I seemed about this time to gain clear sight
Of a new world: a world, too, that was fit
To be transmitted, and to other eyes
Made visible: as ruled by those fixed laws
Whence spiritual dignity originates,
Which do both give it being and maintain
A balance, an ennobling interchange
Of action from within and from without;
The excellence, pure function, and best power
Both of the object seen and eye that sees.

Unhappily the expression ' about this time ', in
line 369, is a vague one. Certainly Wordsworth is not
to be tied by it to the precise time of this tour. If
we attempt so to tie him down, he comes at once into
contradiction with his own words elsewhere. It is clear
that in the lines quoted he intends to say that ' about
this time ' he first began to view nature and man in
connexion, and both as governed by fixed spiritual
laws. Elsewhere, it will be recalled, he has told us that
until the year 1791 Nature remained an exclusive
interest with him, the ' hour of Man ' ' being not yet
come '. The ' hour of Man ' was dominant—and

dominant to the exclusion of Nature—during 1791 and 1792, and the early portion of 1793. From our present passage we infer that somewhere about August 1793 the two interests began for the first time to be balanced. But we shall fall into error, and give to this passage a confused interpretation, if we consider it in isolation. We must read it in the light, above all, of the lines written near Tintern Abbey. Wordsworth visited Tintern immediately after leaving Salisbury Plain; and in the Tintern Poem, written five years afterwards (when he revisited the same scenes with his sister), he describes his feelings as they were in 1793. And ' Nature then ', he says, very definitely, ' Nature then To me was all in all '. Man for the time being was nothing. The feeling for Nature had no need of ' any interest Unborrowed from the eye ' (82).

What is here said of the dominant interest of the faculty of sight is something not said casually. With it should be compared a remarkable passage of the twelfth book of the *Prelude*, which refers to the same period. ' I speak ' Wordsworth says—

> I speak in recollection of a time
> When the bodily eye, in every stage of life
> The most despotic of our senses, gained
> Such strength in me as often held my mind
> In absolute dominion.   (xii. 127–51.)

And again (lines 142 sqq.) :

> Vivid the transport, vivid though not profound,
> I roamed from hill to hill, from rock to rock,
> Still craving combinations of new forms,
> New pleasure, wider empire for the sight,
> Proud of her own endowments, and rejoiced
> To lay the inner faculties asleep.

The same passage describes him as often (in or about the same time)

>   to the moral power,
> The affections and the spirit of the place,
> Insensible.   (xii. 119-21.)

There you have Wordsworth as he was when he visited Tintern in August 1793. The eye is ' the mistress of the heart' (xii. 154). Any interest borrowed from any other sense, or from thought, or from Man, is an intrusion. The exclusion of Man is clearly emphasized in the Tintern poem. It was only during the five years which intervened between the first visit to Tintern and the composition of the poem (on the occasion of the second visit) that the poet learned

> To look on Nature, not as in the hour
> Of thoughtless youth, but hearing oftentimes
> The still sad music of humanity.

We must suppose then that the attitude towards Nature described in *Prelude* xiii. 369 sqq., as developing ' about the time ' of the Salisbury–Tintern tour is, in point of fact, definitely, though not greatly, posterior to it; and that some time shortly after August 1793— but definitely after that date—Wordsworth first began to view Man and Nature in inter-connexion. Yet even so, we must guard against misconception. The manner in which Wordsworth now began to connect Nature and Man is worlds away from the fashion in which that connexion is presented five years later in the Tintern poem. What he now began to connect was Nature and the individual, not, as five years later, Nature and humanity. The voice of humanity does not yet come to him as a ' music ' still and sad, ungrating and free from harshness. It comes to him with the raucous ring of Godwinism. It was at this time that he began to compose *Guilt and Sorrow*; and *Guilt and Sorrow* is, as we shall see in a moment, distinctively Godwinian. What the attitude was of the good Godwinian to Nature we may learn in good prose from Coleridge; from one of the notes prefixed to the poem entitled *France, An Ode*. The ode to France, it may be said in parenthesis, is a valuable commentary upon Wordsworth's revolutionary and Godwinian period: just as the ode on *Dejection* is a valuable commentary upon his supreme period, upon the period culminating in the Immortality ode. 'Those feelings', says Coleridge, 'which the mind attains by its contemplation of its individual nature, and of the sublime surrounding objects (of the external world) do not belong to men as a society, nor can possibly be either gratified or realized under any form of human government; but belong to the individual man, so far as he is pure, and inflamed with the love and adoration of God in Nature'. Leave out what is there said of the love of God, and you have pure Godwinism.

Wordsworth's situation, then, at the time when he began to compose *Guilt and Sorrow*, I take to have been this. In the early part of 1793 humanity and the French Revolution had been his sole interest. He had remained tied to London. He could not bear to face Nature. I have called attention already to the fact that the period February to July is, so far as our knowledge of Wordsworth's feelings and activities are concerned, dark and blank. Save that, at some time during it, he composed his *Apology for the French Revolution* (a work of which the lofty style and sentiment lift it into the first rank of English prose-writings) we know nothing of the manner in which he was occupied. In particular we have no means of conjecturing the antecedents of the sudden revulsion by which, in July of 1793, he broke away from London and buried himself in the country, excluding himself from that close contact with the mighty happenings of the time which, until this month, had seemed a vital necessity to him. We can do no more than barely register an inexplicable mood of utter re-action. A mood pregnant with great consequences. Wordsworth, tearing himself away from London and its vivid pulse of political life, throws himself on Nature, with the passionate addiction of the senses which is described in the Tintern poem and in passages of the twelfth book of the *Prelude*. The rush back to Nature, as it is there described, could be squared with an orthodox Godwinism only by some sophistry. But souls which have anything in them of the primitive are easily, and with dignity, sophistic. As we have seen, Wordsworth shortly before the August of 1793 became startled somehow into the consciousness of a correspondence between the grandeur of Nature and a grandeur in the mind of the individual. Of the individual—it is here that Godwinism holds him. Of humanity in its larger appeal, Nature has as yet nothing to say to him. Nature is the type of grandeur and law and harmony; but Humanity is the Great Anarch. This line of reflection, common, as we have just noticed, to both Wordsworth and Coleridge, seemed to offer the advantage that it reconciled two things in their essence absurdly irreconcilable, Nature and Godwin. Out of the mood resulting from this line of reflection proceeds *Guilt and Sorrow*.

V

GUILT AND SORROW : THE BORDERERS

THE poem brings before us in a solemn setting of desolate natural scenery three utterly desolate, but primitively noble, souls. Of 'humanity' we are reminded only by the swinging chains of a moorland gibbet and the distant prospect of a town-jail. The following may serve for a bare, but perhaps not essentially defective, analysis of the story:

A sailor who, after being taken by the press-gang, had served in Portland Bay during the period of the American Wars, was returning to his wife and family, on demobilization, when he was deprived by fraud of the whole of his small savings. Hitherto he had been the gentlest and best of men, so mild that he would not rob a bird of its food. But now, as he neared his home, the sense of his misfortune brought to him an access of melancholy fury in which he murdered and robbed a traveller. Fleeing from justice, he meets, as he wanders over Salisbury Plain, a woman whom the war has robbed of both husband and children, and who now for three years has lived the life of a vagrant and thief. The two shelter from the storm, and the woman narrates her story to the man. When the storm has abated the two make their way together to a rustic inn, where they are kindly received. While they are there, a country cart arrives, in which lies a woman in the last stages of consumption. This woman explains the circumstances under which she has been driven from her home. A

Guilt and Sorrow: The Borderers

traveller had been found murdered hard by, and suspicion of the crime had fallen upon her absent sailor husband, who had been seen, it was alleged, in the neighbourhood. She protests his innocence, knowing him to be the gentlest and best of men, so mild that he would not rob a bird of its food. Recognition follows, and the husband implores his wife's forgiveness. The wife is by now past speech, but blesses him with a look, and dies. The husband at once surrenders himself to justice, and is hanged.

This may be called a thoroughly Godwinian story. Godwin, in his preface to *St. Leon*, speaking of his novel *Caleb Williams*, says: ' I believed myself fortunate in the selection I had made of the ground-plot of the story: an atrocious crime committed by a man previously of the most exemplary habits.'[1] If Wordsworth himself had prefixed these very words to *Guilt and Sorrow*, they would have been applicable without the change of a letter. The poem was first thought of, as we have seen, in 1793. Wordsworth tells us that it was finished before the close of 1794. Some time in 1794 *Caleb Williams* was published, and I think it is difficult not to believe that the central idea of the plot of *Guilt and Sorrow* is actually derived from the reading of that book. A year later, in the *Borderers*, Wordsworth used again the same idea. In the preface to that play he says, in language which, again, might have come from Godwin himself, that his point of departure has been the ' awful truth ' that ' sin and crime are apt to spring from their opposite qualities '.

But whatever may be the connexion of *Guilt and Sorrow* with *Caleb Williams*, its connexion with God-

[1] Advertisement to *St. Leon*. 1831.

winism is patent. The dominating conception of the poem is essentially necessitarian. The crime of the sailor proceeds from a confused association of ideas, merely; and it is a cardinal doctrine with Godwin that there is no distinct faculty of will, but that what is called will is only 'one of the different cases of the association of ideas'.[1] 'Throw aside your books,' Hazlitt reports Wordsworth as saying, 'and read Godwin on Necessity!' The life, again, of Wordsworth's vagrant woman and her associates, who live by picking and stealing, is not only presented to us as a condition deserving our sympathy, but it recalls a similar glorification of the life of a band of pickpockets in *Caleb Williams*. 'My neighbour', says Godwin in *Political Justice*,[2] 'has just as much a right to put an end to my existence with dagger or poison as to deny me that pecuniary assistance without which I must starve.' Further, *Guilt and Sorrow*, as originally drafted, was without doubt[3] intended to embody a protest against the criminal law generally, and the doctrine of capital punishment in particular. In its present form, however, the poem was not published until 1842, and meantime Wordsworth had given to the world a series of sonnets on the salutary effects of the death penalty. *Guilt and Sorrow* had to be brought into conformity with the Sonnets, and the poet's courageous youth cut according to his uninspired old age. The tame acquiescence in the execution of the sailor, at the end of *Guilt and Sorrow*, was quite certainly not a part of the piece as originally conceived or com-

[1] *Political Justice*², i. 383.

[2] Cited in Harper, i. 258.

[3] 'Its object is partly to expose the vices of the penal law, and the calamities of the war as they affect individuals': Letter to Wrangham, cited in Harper, i. 286.

Guilt and Sorrow : The Borderers

posed. Characteristically Godwinian protests against wealth and property (as the fifth stanza of the *Female Vagrant*),[1] against arms and the profession of arms (the fifteenth stanza), Wordsworth excised in 1842. It is interesting to find Wordsworth in 1794 calling his country's soldiers a ' brood ' that ' dog-like lap their brothers' blood ', and interesting—or rather uninteresting—to find him expunging the passage in 1842. In connexion with this passage, it should be remembered that the pro-French pacifism of the Godwinites in 1793 had its source in the weakening of patriotic feeling which had been brought about by the American War. But finally, and above all, perhaps, the whole social colour of *Guilt and Sorrow*—independently of such individual marks as I have noticed—is Godwinian. The first volume of *Political Justice* contains some bitter sentences which Wordsworth could appropriately have prefixed to *Guilt and Sorrow* as an indication of its general intention. ' Let us survey ', says Godwin, ' the poor, oppressed, hungry, naked . . . man writhing under disease or the fiercer tortures stored up for him by his brethren. . . . Let us plunge into the depths of dungeons.' And then, a characteristically Godwinian touch, ' The evil does not consist merely in the pain endured. It is the injustice which inflicts it that gives it its sharpest sting ' (i. 456). The best life that the peasant can achieve is that of virtue. If he achieve it, he ' is in a certain sense happy ', says Godwin, and then adds the cruellest word in literature—' He is happier than a stone.'

Guilt and Sorrow, then, is a distinctively morbid attack

[1] Stanzas 23-50 of *Guilt and Sorrow* appeared in 1798 under the title *The Female Vagrant*.

upon the whole social order, produced under the influence of Godwinism. It is morbid in its execution; morbid even where real and lively in detail. In its fundamental conception I take it to be, not only unreal, but immoral. It is merely not true. If great crimes and great virtues proceed from one source, if the good man is even more liable than the bad man to bad actions and bad passions, then are we, of all creatures, not only the most miserable, but the most uninteresting. The salt of human drama loses its savour, and what was tragic ceases, in becoming meaningless, to be moving. We shall meet again, in the *Borderers*, this fundamental conception of *Guilt and Sorrow*, and in a form yet more morally perverted, more ingeniously morbid.

The *Borderers* was composed under conditions considerably different from those which gave birth to *Guilt and Sorrow*. Plainly tinged as the earlier poem is with Godwinism, Wordsworth must yet not be regarded as having, at the time at which it was composed, attained the full stature of a Godwinian. He had undergone as yet only a partial initiation. To make this clear, however, it is necessary that we should return for a few moments to his history and movements.

We left him, at line 330 of the tenth book of the *Prelude*, in the Isle of Wight, and with the aid of the thirteenth book we conducted him to Salisbury Plain, and thence to Tintern. The *Prelude* does not give us much help in tracing his further movements. But from his own letters and those of his sister, we can achieve the following rather lacunous reconstruction. By the 30th August 1793 he had reached the end of his western tour, and was with his friend Jones in Wales. From

Guilt and Sorrow : The Borderers

that date until the 17th February 1794, he disappears completely from our knowledge. In February 1794 he was at Halifax with his sister (apparently after some stay with the Calverts in Cumberland). From the 24th May to the 10th January 1795, he was with his sister in the north, mainly in the Cumberland region. Early in 1795 Raisley Calvert died, leaving Wordsworth a bequest which made him independent. But from the beginning of that year until September, we are unable to trace his history. In September 1795, he settled with his sister in Dorset, and there first came under the influence of Coleridge.[1]

What is here said may enable us to draw together the somewhat scattered threads of the relevant portions of the *Prelude*.

From line 331 of Book X to line 52 of Book XI we are occupied with an account (i) of the Terror in France ; (ii) of the death of Robespierre, and the feelings which that event excited in Wordsworth's mind (Leven is mentioned in line 515, and it would follow that at this time he was in the Lake country) ; (iii) the establishment of a milder régime under the Thermidorians or Moderates. The account of the Terror is managed with notable dramatic power, and it has been suggested that the passage is charged with recollections of dangers which were threatening Annette (Annette's family were royalist), and which certainly threatened many persons in France who were bound to Wordsworth by close ties. He conceives the long horror of this time as a kind of ritual of blood and wrath preparing him for the ' after-worship ' of Nature (x. 416–80). In the opening portion, however, of the eleventh book he speaks of the European

[1] This outline relies upon chapters x–xi of Mr. Harper's Life.

situation in a manner clearly not consistent with an out-and-out orthodox Godwinism. Even in depicting the Terror he had used language which implied that he retained, during parts at least of the period of it, an un-Godwinian 'trust in human kind' (x. 388). And the milder time following the death of Robespierre, that of the dominance of the Thermidorians, restored to him, he tells us, an 'unimpaired confidence' in the principles of the Revolution (xi. 7). This confidence he expresses in language which is unmistakably that of a disciple of Rousseau:

> To Nature then
> Power had reverted: habit, custom, law
> Had left an interregnum's open space
> For her to move about in.   (xi. 31-4.)

The interregnum is the period between the death of Robespierre and the establishment of the Directory in the summer of 1795. Wordsworth during that period, though, as *Guilt and Sorrow* has sufficiently shown, he has felt the influence of Godwin somewhat deeply, has not felt it in such a way as to constitute an unhealable breach with the ideal conception of the Revolution which he took from the teaching of Rousseau. By his own account (if I interpret aright a difficult passage) he would have us believe that, up to this point, he has lent to Godwinism only a 'careless ear'. That is, I think, in any case an under-statement; but it is, unless I am mistaken, the right interpretation of lines 188-92 of Book XI of the *Prelude*.

> Meantime,
> As from the first, wild theories were afloat
> To whose pretensions, sedulously urged,
> I had but lent a careless ear, assured
> That time was ready to set all things right.

The 'wild theories' here referred to can, I fancy, only be those of Godwin. They can only be those of Godwin for the reason that they are so carefully contrasted with the view that 'time was ready to set all things right'— they are contrasted, that is, with the Rousseau conception of the Revolution. The essence of Godwinism is precisely its antagonism to the view that 'time was ready to set all things right'. Godwin appeals always from time to eternity—here at least impressive—and from Nature, which is swift, to Reason, which is infinitely slow.

It would appear, therefore, that it was not until the summer of 1795 (after the establishment of the Directory in France) that Wordsworth became a Godwinian to the exclusion of all other forms of belief. The period from the summer of 1793 to that of 1795 is the epoch of what I have called his *semi-Godwinism*. But somewhere about the summer of 1795 his conversion to Godwinism became complete and absolute. The nature of the change, and of the new opinions, is set out with great elaboration in lines 222–319 of the eleventh book of the *Prelude*. Especially significant are lines 238–44. His ambition now is,

> with a resolute mastery shaking off
> Infirmities of nature,[1] time and place,

to

> Build social upon personal liberty;
> Which, to the blind restraints of general laws [2]
> Superior, magisterially adopts
> One guide, the light of circumstances, flashed
> Upon an independent intellect.

Here we have expressed the extreme of Godwinian

[1] i. e. shaking off Rousseauism.
[2] Rousseau's 'general will'.

individualism, the anarchic doctrines that the sole guide of action is the reason of the individual. But where do these lines of the *Prelude* come from? They are borrowed by Wordsworth from his own poem of the *Borderers*, and the *Borderers* was begun in the autumn of 1795 when he settled in Dorset. It was then that Wordsworth first became an out-and-out Godwinian. It is important to arrive at this definition of time,[1] since M. Legouis has argued that the *Borderers* is to be regarded as the beginning of Wordsworth's revolt against Godwin.

Let us now turn to the poem itself. Here is its theme: A perfectly good man, 'the pleasure of all hearts', and enjoying the love of a good woman, took ship to Syria in the reign of Henry III. The crew persuaded him, quite falsely, that the captain was guilty of a plot against his honour. He accordingly lands the captain on a desert shore, leaving him there to starve to death. So far so good. Later, in England, he meets a man the counterpart of himself, a perfectly good man, 'the pleasure of all hearts', enjoying the love of a good woman. He conceives the strange idea of re-creating in this counterpart of himself his own fate. Attaching himself, accordingly, to the company of Borderers commanded by his counterpart, and winning the leader's confidence and affection, he proceeds to poison his mind with suspicions of the father of the girl whom he loves, an old, and blind, and utterly virtuous man. By playing upon his imagination he finally succeeds in persuading him to kill the old man: who is conducted to a desert spot and there left to starve. He is then slain by the other Borderers, and his counterpart,

---

[1] It is additionally guaranteed by *Prelude*, xi. 278, where the words 'free likewise of the world' plainly refer to Wordsworth's situation after he had received the bequest of Raisley Calvert.

Guilt and Sorrow : The Borderers

the virtuous chief of the Borderers, sets out upon a solitary life of wandering penance.

Mr. Swinburne [1] has spoken of the plot of this tragedy as characterized by a 'morbid and monstrous extravagance of horrible impossibility'. Beyond 'the earliest and most frantic romances of Eugène Sue' it is a product of moral disease. 'Il n'y a que les poètes vertueux pour avoir de ces idées-la,' he says, sardonically, quoting a French critic. M. Legouis deprecates this criticism, and we may certainly deprecate the form and manner of it (my citation gives an inadequate notion of its intemperate phrasing). But to M. Legouis, Wordsworth's tragedy is the beginning of a revolt against Godwinism. It is the villain of the *Borderers*, says M. Legouis, who is the Godwinian. It is the villain who, throughout, talks the language of *Political Justice*, and this, Wordsworth means, is what your Godwinism comes to.

That M. Legouis' view can scarcely be sustained follows, I think, from what I have already said of the chronology, generally, of Wordsworth's development and of the circumstances out of which the tragedy was born. But, apart from that, M. Legouis fails to meet the real front of Mr. Swinburne's criticism. Whoever it be who talks the Godwinism in the play, or even if there were no Godwinism talked in it at all, what is really significant, and perhaps alone relevant, is that the poem is built out of an essentially Godwinian idea; the morbid tortuosity, the unnatural perversion of its plot, turns upon a ground-conception patently Godwinian, and that is, after all, the head and front of Mr. Swinburne's attack. Moreover, when M. Legouis tells us that it is the villain who talks Godwinism, I am not sure that the term 'villain' does not beg the

[1] *Miscellanies*, pp. 117 sqq.

question. In so far, in any case, as the villain talks Godwinism, he is not a villain, but a good man. He stands for sheer individualism, and if his individualism ends in disaster, yet Godwin never failed to recognize that individualism, undirected by reason, necessarily perishes. Indeed, reason is the crown of his system—and only so is it that the claim which he made for his book, that it was 'a work from the perusal of which no man should rise without being strengthened in habits of sincerity, fortitude, and justice'[1], is still impressive. The disaster of virtue in the *Borderers* may plausibly be urged to proceed from the fact that both the villain and the hero, though good Godwinians up to a certain point, failed in Godwinism in its first essential. Neither of them followed reason; neither of them asked for evidence and proof at the time of their crime. The whole of Godwinism is a cry for proof. He who does not wait for proof acts against reason: is the creature of impulse.

So far, then, as the disaster which befalls the hero arises from his failure to follow reason, to insist on proof; and so far as that is brought home to us (Wordsworth, I fancy, intended to make it clearer than he has), the tragedy is Godwinian, but not immoral. Its immorality proceeds from its initial conception (as set forth by Wordsworth himself in the preface): the conception that 'sin and crime are apt to spring from their very opposite qualities', and that, a crime once committed, 'there are no limits to the hardening of the heart'. The first part of the thesis is Godwinism, and what is odd is that Wordsworth should still enunciate it in 1842; the second part is an addition of Wordsworth, and either part is wholly false.

[1] *Political Justice*, Preface.

Guilt and Sorrow: The Borderers

I have, in another place, noticed how the initial conception of the play is derived, not mediately from Godwin's philosophy, but immediately from his novel *Caleb Williams*. It should be added here that from *Caleb Williams* is taken also perhaps the idea of laying the scene in a region where there is no law nor established government.

I have mentioned the Godwinian demand for proof. Let us turn back now to that part of the eleventh book of the *Prelude* in which Wordsworth describes his progress in Godwinism. Lines 223-58 describe his gay beginnings; 259-93 his later advances; 293-320 the final goal of disaster. Coming to the period of disaster he says:

> So I fared,
> Dragging all precepts, judgments, maxims, creeds,
> Like culprits to the bar; calling the mind
> Suspiciously to establish in broad day
> Her titles and her honours; now believing,
> Now disbelieving; endlessly perplexed
> With impulse, motive, right and wrong, the grounds
> Of obligation, what the rule, and whence
> The sanction; till, *demanding formal proof*
> *And seeking it in everything*, I lost
> All feeling and conviction, and in fine
> Sick, wearied out with contrarieties,
> Yielded up moral questions in despair.
>   *This was the crisis of that strong disease.*

Swinburne, it would seem, was not so far wrong when he spoke of the *Borderers* as the product of mental disease. He is at least in agreement with Wordsworth himself.

We have now to trace the progress of Wordsworth's recovery: his advance to the period of his supreme and unique strength and health.

vi

ELEMENTS

WORDSWORTH speaks of himself, in his central Godwinian period, as one whose heart had

> been turned aside
> From Nature's way by outward accidents.
> *(Prelude,* xi. 290.)

Whether by 'Nature' he means here the visible beauty of the external world, or that disposition of the human mind and character by which we are farthest from the limitations of custom and nearest to the original goodness which, in accordance with the philosophy of Rousseau, is man's proper possession, does not matter. The two ideas here merge: of our perception of the glory of the external world the precondition is the possession, or the recapture, in ourselves of the original goodness of Man.

So far we have been mainly occupied in tracing the influence upon Wordsworth's mind of other minds than his own. Several names here are of importance: first, Erasmus Darwin (though the *directness* of his influence must appear conjectural); secondly, Rousseau; thirdly, perhaps Beaupuy; and fourthly, William Godwin. In the mirror of one or other of these minds Wordsworth saw all the processes of the French Revolution both as a spiritual and as a political force. Yet another influence was to be added—shortly after the period at which we have arrived—that of Coleridge. Of this last influence I shall say a word or two presently.

Up till now Wordsworth had not attained to self-expression. He had not done so, for the reason that these successive influences had held him back from seeing what he saw with his own eyes, in a truly first-hand fashion. And here we encounter a paradox: for all the while that Wordsworth was trying, through these men's minds, to get at the meaning of the Revolution, he had something in his own experience in which the whole process and meaning of the Revolution was implicit. That is why, despite the many influences to which he submitted his mind, he is ultimately a spirit the most truly original. By which I mean, firstly, that more than other men he has his source in himself; and secondly, in himself, at this source, there was a well, I will not say of unique consciousness, but of consciousness unique in its depth and clearness. From the beginning his consciousness apprehends things in a fashion essentially super-normal. This is perhaps true of all poets, and is what we mean when we speak of their insight and inspiration. We *speak* of these things —whether we really believe in them I do not know. We are apt, I fancy, to apply the term 'inspiration' in a rather figurative fashion: as a kind of courtesy title, conceded in the first instance to the Bible, to save ourselves the trouble of thinking, and for the same reason extended afterwards to anything of apparently cognate quality. But I mean here something very much more definite. I mean that in fact Wordsworth saw things that other people do not see, and that he saw with quite unique clearness and frequency things which they see at most rarely and dimly. This is his originality.

This insight of which I speak may be characterized at once as possessing depth and not breadth. Here is his limitation in comparison with the supreme poets, the super-poets, the men who, like Shakespeare, 'out-top knowledge', the men whom Coleridge, borrowing a phrase from the Neo-Platonists, calls 'myriad-minded'. Wordsworth makes no approach to myriad-mindedness. Not only has he but one mind—I would almost go so far as to say that he has only one idea, and that easily divined.

> There was a boy: ye knew him well, ye cliffs
> And islands of Winander—

and he is perfectly well known to every man, woman, and child of us. Each of us has been he, some time or another. He would stand alone under the trees by the lake-side, and blow mimic hootings to the owls till there was 'concourse wild of jocund din' in the mountain-hollows. And then, as he listened,

> a gentle shock of mild surprise
> Would carry far into his heart the sound
> Of mountain-torrents; or the visible scene
> Would enter unawares into his mind
> With all its solemn imagery, its rocks,
> Its woods, and that uncertain heaven received
> Into the bosom of the steady lake.

Wordsworth's starting-point, the well-head of all his thinking, is either that experience or some one or other variation of it. It may be called a perfectly familiar experience. Each one of us, as I said, can call to mind in his own recollections, analogues to it. It may be called perfectly ordinary. It may equally well be called utterly un-ordinary. In any case, Wordsworth starts always from the fact (guaranteed by at any rate the occasional experience even of the most unimaginative persons), that very often the impression of some natural object or phenomenon, of some familiar incident, an impression simple and purely sensuous, is able to set up a mood of mind or feeling in which the object contemplated is suddenly released from the tie of custom and becomes the source of a mysterious spiritual exaltation. We need not at the moment inquire what is the source of this effect. We can start simply from our experience of it: it does happen. Wordsworth finds the explanation of it in a highly elaborated doctrine of pre-natal reminiscence, and of this doctrine I shall have something to say presently. Meanwhile it is sufficient to start from the fact that, under certain circumstances, objects and incidents the most familiar and natural—the most common, as we say—lose their 'commonness' and set up in us an emotional condition in which we become seized with the greatness of things, their strangeness, a remoteness in them from the clog of matter-of-fact. This may happen in various forms. We may have the sense that we are in the presence of some scene at once new and oddly familiar, that in some remote past we saw and felt all this before. Or we may have the sense that we are contemplating something not substantial, that what we contemplate is in some sort the 'fabric of a vision', and that yet the vision is in some sort more substantial than the things ordinarily so called. These are merely examples from two classes of this order of experience. I take them because these two classes are brought into prominence by Wordsworth, and because, while the experiences involved have been at some time or other known or felt by almost everybody, they were known and felt by Wordsworth in a degree which we must suppose to have been unique, and with a frequency quite beyond the common. I say 'we must suppose': and we must. We shall never understand poets unless we believe what they tell us. It has been said that 'it is the hardest part of interpretation to believe that great men mean what they say'. But it is certainly the most essential part of interpretation. When Wordsworth says that the 'shadowy recollections' of which I speak are 'the fountain light of all his day', a 'master-light of all his seeing'; or when he tells us that, so strong with him, often, in childhood was his sense of the unsubstantiality of familiar objects that he had to hold on to a rock or tree to convince himself that what he saw had existence outside his seeing—when he tells us things like these we are foolish if we do not believe him. We must believe him; and we must believe, as I say, that he possessed a consciousness highly abnormal, to which experiences common to us all, but rare and dim with most, presented themselves with a quite singular frequency and vividness. What the explanation may be of these experiences, put in terms of science, does not here matter. We have to start from the fact of them.

Wordsworth had these experiences at first mostly in connexion with the appearances of what we call 'Nature', and they came to him, not by mental abstraction, but through the senses. That is to say, not only were they the product of 'nature' in the sense of the beauty of the external world, but they were apprehended by that part of the faculties which may be called 'Nature' as distinguished from Reason. Hence he made early the deduction of the natural goodness of the senses. When I say that he made this deduction early, I mean that he made it at an age when he had never heard the name of Rousseau: I mean, indeed, that it was scarcely a deduction. He found it to be so in early childhood, and later years brought nothing to cast doubt upon his

Elements

sense of it. Yet implicit in this is the whole philosophy of Rousseau. I would even go farther and say that there is implicit in it the whole of the French Revolution, and also the whole of Wordsworth's theory of poetry.

Wordsworth observed that the kind of experiences of which we have been speaking had as their characteristic, or as one of their characteristics, that the familiar took on a guise of unfamiliarity: took on, that is to say, a certain newness of aspect. This effect he traced, so far as the mental condition of the beholder was concerned, to an act, or accident, whereby the mind or senses are for the time set free from custom and that tie of habitude which the use of the world binds about us. Upon the ordinary grown man custom lies 'with a weight heavy as frost and deep almost as life'. In early childhood, and in childlike men, the bond is less heavy and intense. But in all cases, it is when custom and matter-of-fact habit drop from us, that we have our truest vision of the world. Nature in Wordsworth is constantly the mere antithesis of custom. It is also often the antithesis of reason, and it is so because he regards reason as in many cases no more than a false effect of custom. When we fail to see what is unfamiliar in the familiar, that is because custom obtrudes itself; alternatively, we may express this by saying that reason and its complexity obstructs the pure and simple work of the senses.

Wordsworth starts, then, from the position not only that Nature is good, but that it is from the natural goodness of the senses, operating simply and directly, that we derive ' the fountain-light of all our day '. We get farthest from the source of things the nearer we draw to all that in life is complex and artificial. Wherever we have things and persons whom chance, or the order of the world, has kept free from the bond of custom, has left simple and not complex, there we may look for illumination upon the things that really matter —the things that matter to the soul. It is thus that the child and the peasant become to Wordsworth the types of a wisdom higher than that of the world. He even goes farther. He is prepared to find insight and inspiration in the mad, the crazed, and the idiotic. We are apt to attribute this penchant in him for Bedlamites, imbeciles, and 'simples' to mere childish whim. Yet, however perverse it may be, it is in fact a most solid part of his theory of life and of the mind and of truth.

All the doctrines of the French Revolution are here implicit: its demand for the free development, in the individual, of nature; its demand for political simplification; its war upon custom; its attack upon class distinctions: its conception of a kingdom of heaven, here and now, for those who can exchange the prejudices of grown men for the faith of little children. This is how it comes about that Wordsworth, as I have already noticed, insists that the French Revolution, in its first aspects, left him tranquil and almost unconcerned, for the reason that it seemed to him the most natural thing in the world.

Literary theory followed the same way. The beginning of style, like the beginning of spiritual insight—of which if it is not the voice, it is mere babbling—is to loose hold of convention and artificiality. The child and the peasant are not only the true seers, they are at the same time the only stylists. Here is a vast world of literary theory, in connexion with which I will make only one suggestion— which is capable of being applied outside Wordsworth's theory of style to all that part of his thinking which bases upon the doctrine that simplicity is found in lowliness. So far as I understand the things that anthropologists tell us, it would appear that the farther back we go in our study of primitive types, the more do we discover a paradox in the primitive mind which impels it to operate in every way save that which is direct and obvious. In some aspects the savage is more a metaphysician than the most befogged of modern philosophers, and in general, wherever his deepest beliefs are involved, his mind is found to be the most tortuous conceivable. And his style—if one may speak of style in such a connexion—his style follows suit. He does not talk by nature, but by the rules of an intricate system of magic. He of all men is most in love with formulas, which to those not bred in them have no significance whatever. Wordsworth was not wholly unaware of this himself. At the end of the third book of the *Excursion* the Solitary describes how he voyaged to America supposing that he would find there man in his pure and simple elements. But that pure archetype, he says,

                              of human greatness
—I found him not. There in his stead appeared
A creature squalid, vengeful and impure,
Remorseless and submissive to no law
But superstitious fear and abject sloth.

The passage opens up infinite avenues of ingenious speculation. *Sed me terrent vestigia.* Who goes this path must meet and slay (for which I am not strong enough) the paradox that simplicity, far from being a wild-flower plant, is the supreme creation, the grand culminating product, of that hot-house of hybrid effects which we call civilization.

vii

EYES AND EARS

WE have followed, in close detail, the process by which Wordsworth was 'turned away from Nature' by the 'outward accidents' of the Revolution, and the further process of alienation induced by a false philosophy. That we have been enabled to do this, we owe, in the main, to Wordsworth himself. But neither Wordsworth himself, nor external sources, suffice to enable us to trace in similar detail the process of restoration and reconcilement. Wordsworth's account of it, in the last books of the *Prelude*, is at once diffuse and uninforming. It may be doubted whether in the indications which he furnishes he is always quite consistent with himself, and towards a chronology of the process of restoration he contributes nothing. The *Borderers* was finished in 1796, a product of mental and moral disease. The *Lyrical Ballads* appeared in 1798, and even if, among them, is included the *Female Vagrant*, yet as a whole they present to us a radiant and settled health of genius. Indeed, whatever is new and wonderful in the *Lyrical Ballads*, nothing is more wonderful than that they should have come from the Wordsworth whom we have hitherto known. They usher in, without any forewarning, a swift springtime of clear song. Without preparation we pass at once from a condition drearily morbid to a puissant and settled serenity.

In Wordsworth's own account there were three principal agents in the work of restoration: his sister Dorothy, Mary Hutchinson (whom he married in 1802),

Eyes and Ears

and Coleridge.[1] The passage in which the three are thus associated dates from 1806, and it is reasonable to conceive the influence of Mary Hutchinson as having been, in the main, only confirmatory. The original restoration, as accomplished some time during 1797, is the work of the poet's sister and of Coleridge. With regard to the former, Wordsworth is not quite consistent. In the Tintern poem, Dorothy's communion with Nature is represented (in 1798) as made up of 'wild ecstasies', presently to be 'matured into a sober pleasure', such a 'sober pleasure' as the poet has himself already learnt to feel—at present she is still, in her perception of Nature, what Wordsworth himself was in 1793; he beholds in her 'what once he was' himself, the as yet untamed enthusiast of natural beauty. In the *Prelude*, on the other hand (xiv. 243–67), it is Dorothy from whom Wordsworth himself first learnt to tame a 'soul too reckless of mild grace', too prone to seek the beauty which has terror in it. She is described as 'a kind of gentler spring' going before his steps in the period in which he was learning to catch, in the accents of Nature,

> The still, sad music of humanity,
> Nor harsh, nor grating, though of ample power
> To chasten and subdue.

Whether the later or the earlier of these two pictures of Dorothy Wordsworth be the true one it seems not possible to determine. The discrepancy (to which, so far as I know, attention has not before been directed) is noteworthy; and I will only suggest that, in considering it, we should do well to bear in mind that Wordsworth himself, as we have already seen, believed

[1] *Prelude*, xiv. 232–301.

that he wrote most truly when he wrote at a distance from his original impressions.

The influence of Coleridge [1] was an influence certainly not less potent than any other; and the more closely we study Wordsworth, the more dominant, I think, we shall feel this influence to have been.

Wordsworth seems to conceive his restoration as consisting mainly in a free re-surrender to natural influences: in the unresisting re-immersion in Nature of a self hardened by a four years sophistication. The system of Godwin had left no room in the world for sense, passion, will, imagination, sympathy, habit. From this self-defeating extreme of Rationalism Wordsworth seems to recede, not by any logical process, nor by gradations, but suddenly; by a rush of conflicting feeling, by the unpredictable melting of a proud and prodigal temperament. With never a word, he lays his head again in the lap of Nature. A mysterious resurgence of the primaeval carries him from deep to deep. *Die Mütter, die Mütter; es klingt so wunderlich!* Somewhat thus the return seems to be made. But can Nature keep her child? Let us see.

I have said that Wordsworth possessed originality in the sense in which that word is most properly used; in the sense, that is, firstly, that he had his source in himself, and secondly, that at this source he drew upon a consciousness unique in depth and clearness. The primary elements of this consciousness are few and simple. Wordsworth sets out always, I said, from impressions common to himself and to you and me, but

---

[1] In the summer of 1797 Coleridge was engaged on 'a book of morals in answer to Godwin' (J. Dykes Campbell: *S. T. Coleridge*, p. 77).

felt by him in a fashion quite abnormal in respect both of their quality and their frequency. He so sees objects as, in the act of contemplating them, to release them from the tie of custom, from their ' commonness ', their familiarity. The old becomes new, the substantial visionary. I use the word ' visionary ' advisedly, for it brings us at once to the central paradox of Wordsworth's poetry. Wordsworth's poetry is essentially mystical. But whereas the mysticism of other men consists commonly in their effort to escape from the senses, the mysticism of Wordsworth is grounded and rooted, actually, *in* the senses. The natural world speaks, not to the intellect, but to that in us which is most ' natural ', viz. our senses. It is only when we allow reason, or intellect, to confuse the clear and sweet report of the senses that we cease to see visions, and from being poets become mere men again. It is our eyes and our ears that matter to us ; it is by them that we become wise and immortal—as soon as we begin to think, we join the foolish or the dead. If Wordsworth does not go so far as to tell us that ' the soul is but the senses catching fire ', he at least comes near to hinting it. I say ' Wordsworth ', and I mean by that the Wordsworth who now discovers himself to us in *Lyrical Ballads*; not the Godwinian Wordsworth, truly ; nor yet the Wordsworth who in later life spoke of ' I and my brother the Dean ' ; but the Wordsworth who matters, the Wordsworth who begins in 1798 and dies about 1807. This pure sensationalism of Wordsworth —I use ' sensationalism ', of course, in its philosophic sense, of a theory of mind which regards the senses as the source of truth—this pure sensationalism of Wordsworth is apt to take us by surprise. It surprises us because (as I have said earlier) we are not much in the habit of believing that poets mean what they say. And certainly, in its implications, it appears, at least to our first reflections, a degree naïve. Yet in this sensationalism Wordsworth began, and it is when he passes from it (about 1807) that he ends. He began in it—it goes back to those first beginnings of poetry in him which he so much delights to trace in the *Prelude*, calling up one image after another of his inspired childhood. He began in it, and then, for a brief period, his heart was 'turned aside'; and then, in 1798, he began in it again. But with a difference. The true significance of the period of his restoration lies in the fact that in 1798, with the aid, as I think, of Coleridge, he placed his sensationalism upon a new basis; and it is of the first importance that we should understand the character of the new foundations upon which he built. I asked, 'Can Nature keep her child?' Wordsworth felt the same misgivings. Let us see how he (and Coleridge) endeavoured, and with what success, to allay them.

The sensationalism of *Lyrical Ballads* may be described as not merely frank but proselytising. Nature is not on the defensive, but she is set to carry an offensive campaign into the capital of Reason. Everywhere she is out to harry the 'meddling intellect'.

> Sweet is the lore which nature brings,
>   Our *meddling intellect*
> Misshapes the beauteous forms of things,
>   We murder to dissect.

That is from the poem entitled *The Tables Turned*, and it is interesting from the fact that there is ground for supposing that the person addressed is William Hazlitt; but certainly Hazlitt was no pedantic enthusiast of

Reason. There is the same tilting against the intellect when the poet addresses his sister on 'the first mild day of March':

> One moment now may give us more
> Than years of *toiling reason*.

The antithesis of Nature and Intellect gives the keynote, again, of the *Poet's Epitaph*. The Poet is one

> Contented if he may enjoy
> The things that others *understand*;

and, in the same poem, the Moralist is described as one in whom self-absorption has killed the senses—he is one who 'hath neither eyes nor ears'; whereas the riches of the Poet are

> The harvest of a quiet eye
> That broods and sleeps on his own heart.

This gospel of eyes and ears intrudes itself, indeed, at all points:

> The eye—it cannot choose but see;
> We cannot bid the ear be still.[1]

The examples I have offered are taken, it is true, from poems somewhat slight in form and character. But the same gospel reveals itself in a poem of a quite different species; a poem marked by a high degree of elaboration, which is indeed Wordsworth's first essay in philosophic poetry—the lines written at Tintern in 1798. This poem, in the first edition of *Lyrical Ballads*, was given the place of honour. We know from one of Wordsworth's letters [2] that it was his habit to place at the end of each volume that poem in it to which he wished principally to direct attention. *Lyrical Ballads* ends with the Tintern poem. The poem is the crown and coping stone of the *Lyrical*

[1] *Expostulation and Reply*, 17–18.   [2] Grosart, iii, p. 349.

Ballads, and it may still perhaps be regarded as containing more of the pure gospel of Wordsworth than anything else which he wrote.

> For I have learned
> To look on nature, not as in the hour
> Of thoughtless youth, but hearing oftentimes
> The still sad music of humanity,
> Nor harsh nor grating, though of ample power
> To chasten and subdue. And I have felt
> A presence that disturbs me with the joy
> Of elevated thoughts; a sense sublime
> Of something far more deeply interfused,
> Whose dwelling is the light of setting suns,
> And the round ocean and the living air,
> And the blue sky, and in the mind of man:
> A motion and a spirit which impels
> All thinking things, all objects of all thought,
> And rolls through all things. Therefore am I still
> A lover of the meadows and the woods,
> And mountains; and of all that we behold
> From this green earth; of all *the mighty world
> Of eye and ear*,—both what they half create,
> And what perceive; well pleased to recognize
> *In nature and the language of the sense*
> The anchor of my purest thoughts, the nurse,
> The guide, the guardian of my heart, and soul
> Of all my moral being.   (88–111.)

Note here 'the mighty world of eye and ear'—it is the only world. The poem is addressed to the poet's sister, and it is of her that he says elsewhere that 'she gave me eyes, she gave me ears'[1]—the only gifts for which he had any use. But above all, note the lines where with deliberation, and beyond the chances of misunderstanding, Wordsworth tells us that he recognizes in Nature and the report of sense, not merely the

The Sparrow's Nest, 17–18.

guide of feeling and of the heart, but the 'soul of all his moral being'.

Only a few years before he had spoken of himself, in the crisis of his Godwinian period, as ' yielding up moral questions in despair '. Now in ' eyes and ears ' he finds the answer to all moral questions.

It is the essence of the critical spirit—it is the essence of rationalism—that in the long run it defeats itself. Wordsworth had pursued Godwinism to a point where it was discovered to wash vainly against the high shores of Nature and of human nature. In the twelfth book of the *Prelude* (104 sqq.) he describes how the critical spirit had stood between him and Nature; and in the thirteenth book (215–20) how the same spirit, over-emphasizing the division which life makes between man and man, had shut him off from the ' universal heart '. This critical spirit is answered, so far as Nature is concerned, by eyes and ears. In the long run, no criticism can stand up against eyes and ears. It is answered again, so far as man is concerned, by the fact of the affections. Godwin had cast out the affections with a pitchfork, and now they came running back. With this matter of the affections I am not at the moment concerned. I am concerned only with Wordsworth's conception of Nature and of the action of natural objects upon the soul. His doctrine here is, as I say, a doctrine of pure sensationalism. But does it hold? Can Nature keep her child?

I have already given some hint of the manner in which Wordsworth (helped perhaps by the metaphysic of Coleridge) was prepared to answer the obvious criticisms which a naïve sensationalism provokes. The grand repositories of truth are eyes and ears. But sense, for

Wordsworth, always points us beyond sense. Its light is what, in the *Ode*, he calls a '*visionary* gleam'. We have already observed how, in the sixth book of the *Prelude* (599–602), he finds the characteristic of the highest sense perception to be that, in the very act itself of seeing,

> the light of sense
> Goes out, but with a flash that has revealed
> The invisible world.

Similarly, in the Tintern poem, he tells us that in the deeper moods of contemplation, though we use the bodily senses, yet there is a serene and exalted condition of sensuous apprehension wherein

> we are laid asleep
> In body, and become a living soul. (45–6.)

The senses always report more than they see. But they do so only if we leave them to themselves. If we thrust in our thinking, if we intrude the 'meddling intellect', we miss the 'visionary gleam'; the 'glory and the dream' wither and are lost.

> Nor less I deem that there are Powers
>   Which of themselves our minds impress;
> That we can feed this mind of ours
>   In a wise passiveness.
>
> Think you, 'mid all this mighty sum
>   Of things for ever speaking,
> That nothing of itself will come,
>   But we must still be seeking?

But even so, have we sufficiently safeguarded nature? And has Wordsworth's sensationalism answered all questions which he, or we, can ask of it?

Two vital questions press for an answer; questions of the force and direction of both of which Wordsworth was fully—we might even say painfully—conscious. First, what does it mean when sense points beyond sense? What is the source of this something in sight and sound which makes the common things of earth perpetually new and strange, and which hints immortality to us? Secondly, in the natural decay which years bring, when either the individual senses lose their keenness, or the spirit to which they report sheds its freshness, how can we arrest and stay the ' vision ' by which we live? Or, as the vision fades and fails, what new source of life and truth, if any, is opened to us?

These two questions Wordsworth endeavours to answer for us in many places, notably in the latter books of the *Prelude* and in what Coleridge calls ' the immortal Ode on Immortality '. I propose to take the *Ode* as embodying Wordsworth's systematized reflection upon the themes I have mentioned, and to submit this great masterpiece to an examination in some detail.

viii

THE 'IMMORTAL ODE'

It is worth while first to reconstruct the circumstances in which the *Ode* was written. It was begun in the spring of 1802. Wordsworth was at Dove Cottage, with his sister. Coleridge had just returned to the Lake Country and had paid them a visit at Grasmere. That was on 18–20th March. The importance of Coleridge's presence will appear shortly. On 22nd March Dorothy Wordsworth records in her journal that, on a mild morning, William ' worked at the Cuckoo poem '; and again on 25th March ' A beautiful morning. W. worked at the Cuckoo '. Then on the next day: ' William wrote to Annette, then worked at the Cuckoo . . .' in the evening ' he wrote the *Rainbow* '. I will try and indicate in a moment the significance of these poems in relation to the *Ode*. On the day following, 27th March, ' Wm. wrote part of an Ode '—this was *the* Ode. Later, 17th June, ' Wm. added a little to the Ode he is writing '.

First the *Cuckoo*. This is the poem placed second among the Poems of the Imagination.[1] The voice of the cuckoo brings to Wordsworth ' a tale Of *visionary* hours '—a tale of days of childhood when the cuckoo was ' an invisible thing, a voice, a mystery '. As he hears him now again, once more suddenly the earth ' appears to be An unsubstantial faery place That is meet home for thee '. He is back in the world of those

---

[1] I mention that because the poem is in form somewhat slight and fanciful. Wordsworth placed it where it is because to him it was neither.

visionary experiences of childhood which he regarded as the source of the deepest illumination.

He had no sooner finished the *Cuckoo* than he began upon the *Rainbow*. The sight of the rainbow still brings to him the old 'leaping up of the heart' which he had as a boy. He prays that it may always continue to be so:

> The child is father of the man
> And I could wish my days to be
> Bound each to each by natural piety.

In the edition of 1815 these lines are prefixed as a motto to the *Ode*. There is the external link, that they were composed contemporaneously with it. But there is an inner connexion, the significance of which has, I think, not been fully apprehended. In the first place it has, I fancy, not been pointed out that, when in lines 22-3 of the *Ode* Wordsworth says

> To me alone there came a thought of grief:
> A timely utterance gave that thought relief,

the timely utterance may very well be the Rainbow poem itself. Secondly, the conception of human days bound together by natural piety is the clue to the interpretation of the *Ode* in its entirety. I shall try to make this clear as we proceed.

The *Ode*, so far as it was carried at this time, ended with the fourth stanza; and was not completed in its entirety until 1806. This we know from Wordsworth's own statement in the Fenwick Notes—though we must not necessarily suppose, I think, that fragments and scraps of the later stanzas had not taken at least inchoate form at the earlier date. But so far as it was a complete piece in 1802, it ended with lines 56-7:

> Whither is fled the visionary gleam?
> Where is it now, the glory and the dream?

It is not, I think, accident that the poem broke off thus at this unanswered question: that between the question and the answer there intervenes a period of no less than four years. We are here, I am inclined to suppose, brought up against a crisis, a turning-point, in Wordsworth's intellectual development. Until now he has lived in 'the glory and the freshness' of the senses, in the immediate report given by the senses of a 'principle of joy' in the world. But with advancing years this report comes to be fitful and dim. 'The things that I have seen I now can see no more.'

What does that mean? How does that happen? And, if it happens, as it does, what is the meaning and value, as against the early gift of vision, of the 'years which bring the philosophic mind'?

Wordsworth, as I have said, undoubtedly had these visionary experiences in great intensity both of number and quality. Undoubtedly they were to him the most real and valuable thing in life. We may shrug our shoulders, but so it was; and we must start out from that. We shall not understand him unless we attune ourselves to his mood, which is, for him, one of philosophy and not fancy. Examples of a fanciful expression of the same mood occur of course in many places in literature.

> Sing me a song of a lad that is gone,
> Say, could that lad be I?
> Merry of soul he sailed on a day,
> Over the sea to Skye.
> Give me again all that was there,
> Give me the sun that shone!
> Give me the eyes, give me the soul,
> Give me the lad that's gone!

But Stevenson's pretty poem takes us to, and keeps us in, a wholly different world. Wordsworth is propounding to us with all the seriousness of which he is capable a question which has not merely crossed his fancy but which is for him the central question of the imaginative life.

The first four stanzas of the *Ode* put the fact : ' There hath passed a glory from the earth ' ; and in the last two lines of them, ask the explanation of it. Stanzas v–viii give the explanation in the form of the doctrine of *anamnesis* or Reminiscence. Stanzas ix–xi are an attempt to vindicate the value of a life from which ' vision ' has fled.

The ultimate source of the doctrine of reminiscence is, of course, Plato and the Neo-Platonists. The immediate source, however, upon which Wordsworth drew can hardly be in doubt. It was not Plato, but Coleridge. Here are the opening lines of a sonnet written by Coleridge, in 1796, on receiving intelligence of the birth of a son (the son was Hartley Coleridge) :

Oft o'er my brain does that strong fancy roll
Which makes the present (while the flash doth last)
Seem a mere semblance of some unknown past,
Mixed with such feelings as perplex the soul
Self-questioned in her sleep ; and some have said
We lived ere yet this robe of flesh we wore.

In a note appended to this sonnet Coleridge refers merely to Plato. In a letter, however, to his friend Poole, he seems to indicate Fénelon as his nearest source. ' Almost all the followers ', he says, ' of Fénelon believe that men are degraded intelligences, who had all once lived together in a paradisiacal, or perhaps heavenly, state. The first four lines express a feeling which I have often had—the present has appeared like a vivid dream or exact similitude of some past circumstances.' That

Wordsworth drew upon Coleridge is indicated, not only by the general consideration of his philosophic indebtedness to Coleridge, but also by the fact that the first hint in him of the reminiscence doctrine occurs (as it occurs in Coleridge) in connexion with Hartley Coleridge—in the opening line of the verses *To H. C., Six Years Old*:

O thou whose fancies from afar are brought.

These verses are usually said to have been composed in 1802. But they are quoted by Coleridge in *Anima Poetae* (p. 15) under the date 1801, at a time when Hartley was only four years old. Look now at lines 85-6 of the Immortality Ode:

Behold the child among his new-born blisses,
A six years' darling of a pigmy size.

The first edition has ' a four years' darling '. I cannot help thinking that the child depicted in the *Ode* is actually Hartley Coleridge; that there is a close connexion between the two poems, and that in both Wordsworth, at a later date, altered 'four' to 'six', as more suited to the habits and disposition ascribed to the child. In any case we may, I think, without improbability regard Coleridge as the source from which the reminiscence doctrine took rise in Wordsworth's imagination. That being so, it is interesting to find Coleridge, in that part of the *Biographia Literaria* where he speaks of the *Ode on Immortality*, warning the reader against taking Wordsworth's doctrine of pre-existence in the literal and ' ordinary interpretation '. ' The Ode ', he says,

' was intended for such readers only as had been accustomed to watch the flux and reflux of their inmost nature, to venture at times into the twilight realms of consciousness, and to feel a deep interest in modes of inmost being, to which they know that the attributes of time and space are inapplicable and alien, but which can yet not be conveyed, save in symbols of time and space. For such readers the sense is sufficiently plain, and they will be as little disposed to charge Mr. Wordsworth with believing the Platonic pre-existence in the ordinary interpretation of the words, as I am to believe that Plato himself ever meant or taught it!'

Wordsworth himself in later life was somewhat concerned as to the use to which he had put the doctrine. Yet what he is concerned about is, not that the doctrine may not be true, but that it may be intrusive; that it is not a part of the teaching of the Church, and may be misconceived as qualifying, or superseding, that teaching.[1] Nothing that he says anywhere suggests that he entertained the doctrine otherwise than seriously; and this is only another of the cases where, as I have said, we shall not understand him unless we believe what he tells us. I am no more in doubt that Wordsworth believed the doctrine than I doubt that Plato did—Coleridge's scepticism, it will be noticed, extends even to Plato.[2]

But for Wordsworth, it should be made clear, the doctrine has both a different foundation and a different significance from that which it has in Plato. Wordsworth, as I have said, is a pure sensationalist. Plato, on the other hand, is a pure intellectualist. To Plato the doctrine of reminiscence is a theory of knowledge: an explanation of how we get to know and think. The senses are the source of all error. The world of 'Ideas'

[1] Grosart, iii, pp. 194-5.
[2] Coleridge, in a late piece, *Phantom or Fact*, draws again on the doctrine.

alone has truth. It is only by escape from the contamination of the senses, only by getting away from eyes and ears, that we are able truly to see and hear, and to come to the truth of things. The process is a long and painful labour of abstraction. But to Wordsworth the truth of things comes in flashes, in gleams of sense-perception; and in abstraction the truth dies. Wordsworth's doctrine is, in fact, not a theory of knowledge, but a romance of sensation. The absorbing interest of Plato is in the logical meanings of things; to Wordsworth logical meanings are precisely that part of things which has no value. There is some degree of delusion, therefore, in speaking of the Platonism of Wordsworth; and if we are to read the *Ode* rightly we shall do well to begin by putting Plato out of our minds.

Our pre-natal existence is guaranteed for Plato by the fact that we can reason at all; by the power in us to form class-conceptions. It is guaranteed to Wordsworth by a passivity of response to sense-impressions; and in this connexion I feel obliged to reiterate what I have already said in another connexion. In considering the character of the impressions made upon Wordsworth by Nature, we must conceive ourselves always, I believe, to be dealing with impressions made upon a consciousness highly abnormal. The flashes thrown by sense on the invisible world came to him with a frequency and fullness of illumination not given to ordinary men. And just as his experience here is not ordinary, so I conceive it to be not ordinary in respect of that phenomenon which is the main theme of the *Ode*—in respect of the manner in which, as we pass from childhood to youth, and from youth to manhood, the flashes of vision become ever more and more faint and intermittent.

That this is what happened in Wordsworth's own case it is not possible to doubt. He tells us so; he reiterates it; we may even say that it is a chief trouble of his soul— for the things that are thus passing from him are precisely the things which he regards as more precious than anything else in life. Yet so far as we can judge, so far as general report can be trusted, Wordsworth's experience in this particular is not that of ordinary men. One is tempted to the conjecture that the extraordinary force and frequency of the visionary experiences of his earlier years exhausted prematurely—actually wore out by over-use—the faculty of vision itself. In the *Ode*, and elsewhere, Wordsworth endeavours to persuade himself —and us—that he has replaced this visionary gift by some other gift or gifts; that he still draws upon sources of experience not inferior in depth and clearness. But *does* he? In all that matters to us, that is to say in his poetry, does he? The great *Ode* closes the two volumes of 1807. Why is it that thereafter we pass into the dark, or, at any rate, out of the fullness of light, that we are conscious that, 'where e'er we go', 'there hath passed a glory' from his poetry, and that the things which we have seen with his eyes, we 'now can see no more'? In this early decay of a faculty abnormally developed and abnormally employed I am inclined (leaving the faculty itself unexplained in its origin and nature) to seek at least a partial explanation of the extraordinary decline in poetic power which begins with the ending of the *Ode*. Wordsworth did cease to see things.

This is not, of course, an explanation which will satisfy any one who supposes that Wordsworth was like other people; that 'inspiration' is a metaphor, and the epithet 'seer' a courtesy title. For myself, when poets

tell me that they are inspired, I am disposed to believe
them—I have found it always the shortest way, not only
of placating them, but of understanding them. It may
even be that it is the only way.

There are two passages of Wordsworth which should
always be read in connexion with the *Ode*; and in both
of which we have a somewhat pathetic expression of his
sense of lost vision. Of these the first is to be found in
the concluding portion of the twelfth book of the
Prelude—I have already quoted the opening lines of it:

> O mystery of man, from what a depth
> Proceed thy honours. I am lost, but see
> In simple childhood something of the base
> On which thy greatness stands; but this I feel
> That from thyself it comes, that thou must give,
> Else never canst receive. The days gone by
> Return upon me almost from the dawn
> Of life: the hiding-places of man's power
> Open: *I would approach them, but they close.*
> *I see by glimpses now; when age comes on,*
> *May scarcely see at all;* and I would give,
> *While yet we may*, as far as words can give,
> Substance and life to what I feel, enshrining,
> Such is my hope, the spirit of the past
> For future restoration.   (xii. 272–86.)

The words which I have put into italics are sufficiently
significant to stand without comment. The passage was
composed about the time at which the *Ode* was brought
to completion. By the side of it may be set a stanza of
the *Ode composed upon an Evening of extraordinary
Splendour and Beauty*: a poem written in 1818:[1]

> Such hues from their celestial urn
> Were wont to stream before mine eye,

---

[1] No. ix of the *Evening Voluntaries*; but not an original part of
that series (which dates as a whole from 1833: Grosart, iii. 145).

> Where'er it wandered in the morn
> Of blissful infancy.
> This glimpse of glory, why renewed?
> Nay, rather speak with gratitude;
> For if a vestige of those gleams
> Survived, 'twas only in my dreams.
> Dread Power, whom peace and calmness serve
> No less than Nature's threatening voice,
> From THEE if I would swerve;
> O, let thy grace remind me of the light
> Full early lost, and fruitlessly deplored;
> Which at this moment on my waking sight
> Appears to shine, by miracle restored;
> My soul, though yet confined to earth,
> Rejoices in a second birth!
> 'Tis past, the visionary splendour fades;
> And night approaches with her shades.   (61–80.)

When Wordsworth speaks here of

> the light
> Full early lost, and fruitlessly deplored,

it is the same light as that of which he speaks in the *Ode on Immortality* as 'the fountain-light of all our day' and 'the master-light of all our seeing'. And when he speaks of this light as 'fruitlessly deplored', it can hardly be but that the reference in those words is to the great *Ode* itself; and we must suppose Wordsworth to have had the sense that the *Ode*, great as it is, was great in a somewhat 'fruitless' fashion; that, philosophically, it failed; that it did not answer adequately the questions which it set out to solve. When I say 'adequately', I mean adequately from the point of view which Wordsworth had reached in 1818. By that date he had reached a theistic position which the *Evening Voluntaries*, as a whole, reflect. Nature is no longer identified with God or the divine; but God is conceived in an external relation, as the creator of Nature; and our perception of Nature and its glory we owe, no longer to the free senses, but to 'Grace'. Grace 'reminds us of the light'. Similarly in the fourth of the *Evening Voluntaries*, By grace divine, he says,

> By grace divine,
> Not otherwise, O Nature, we are thine,
> Through good and evil, thine.   (16-18.)

To such a mood the great *Ode* must necessarily appear a 'fruitless' achievement.

But if we get away from the Wordsworth of 1818, and look at the *Ode* from the point of view of the Wordsworth of 1797-1807, we have still to ask, Whether it achieves its end, whether it is, in fact, successful in vindicating a life no longer, or only rarely, visited by these 'visionary gleams' which belong to the fullness and purity of the free senses. The vindication of such a life is attempted in the last three stanzas of the poem. The ninth stanza begins, or purports to begin, on a note of gladness:

> O joy, that in our embers
> Is something that doth live!

Even so, it is not a very auspicious beginning. The fire of joy seems, after all, to be not more than a spark among the smouldering embers of a dying life. It is just 'something that doth live', a something better than nothing in a decolorated and frigescent world. Nor is this living *something*, in the dying embers of Wordsworth's imagination, readily or easily apprehensible. At first sight, he would appear to tell us no more than that the loss of light is adequately compensated by the recollection of it. That is certainly something not consistent with ordinary human experience—we were happy indeed were it possible for us in the lean years of life to fill the empty granaries of the heart by thinking upon more kindly summers. But neither is it possible, nor is it likely that it appeared so to Wordsworth.

What, then, is he really trying to say to us in the last three stanzas of the *Ode*?

In order to answer this question satisfactorily, it is necessary that, in conjunction with Wordsworth's speculations upon nature and the goodness of Nature, we should consider to some extent also his view of certain aspects of the moral life. I have said that the lines from the Rainbow poem, prefixed to the *Ode*, were intended to serve, as I thought, as a clue to the poem. The child is father of the man, Wordsworth there says,

> And I could wish my days to be
> Bound each to each by natural piety.

The idea here put to us is illustrated, rather unexpectedly, in a poem of a quite different character—the *Happy Warrior*. The Happy Warrior is described as one who,

> when brought
> Among the tasks of real life, hath wrought
> Upon the plan that pleased his childish thought.

The Happy Warrior is, in fact, one who has bound his days together. He has so bound up his life that the pure and free impressions of childhood, its visionary experiences, are the inspiration of his mature age. The poem takes us from the natural to the moral world; but the principle at issue is the same, nor does Wordsworth part these two worlds so sharply as we do. The principle is further illustrated, in its purely moral aspect, in the *Ode to Duty*:

> There are who ask not if thine eye
> Be on them; who in love and truth,
> Where no misgiving is, rely
> Upon the genial strength of youth:
> Glad hearts without reproach or blot,
> Who do thy work and know it not.
> Long may the kindly influence last;
> But thou, if they should totter, teach them to stand fast!

I doubt whether Wordsworth, in his best period, ever abandoned the doctrine that the highest moral achievement is that which presents itself as an inspiration, that which is part of our natural life, that which is bound up with childhood and its unthinking 'vision'. Duty is a second-best; we seek support from that power when higher and freer powers fail us. The purer moral life is that which so binds together our days that the vision of childhood suffices to later years.[1]

---

[1] We may profitably conceive the *Prelude*, accordingly, as a self-examination directed towards binding together the poet's own days, his different periods, and moments, of inspired consciousness.

ix
SENSE AND IMAGINATION

On the side, then, of Nature Wordsworth finds the highest and deepest truth in the pure report of the senses, unspoiled by reason; on the side of morality, he finds the highest virtue in a natural goodness unspoiled by the calculations of Duty.

But with advancing years, first, the vision which the senses have of Nature, and secondly the instinct of natural goodness for right action, may alike fail. How may this failure be stayed? and what, in either case, do the 'years which bring the philosophic mind' supply to us in the place of what we lose?

Natural virtue is replaced by duty. That is clear enough: 'we seek thy firm support according to our need', he says to Duty. We might expect that the senses would be replaced by Reason or Intellect. But this sudden intrusion of the intellect, the 'meddling intellect' against which Wordsworth has so long contended, and in so spirited a fashion—this disloyalty to all first principles—is clearly intolerable and incredible. It is not even true that Wordsworth replaces natural virtue by duty. He does so in words; but in the act of doing it, he gives to 'duty' a new signification. Duty to Wordsworth is no mere reasoning faculty, cold, calculative, hesitant. When he says of Duty,

> Thou dost wear
> The godhead's most benignant grace,
> Nor know we anything so fair
> As is the smile upon thy face;

when he speaks thus of Duty, it is clear that he has taken us out of the world of calculation and hesitancies into a world of pure imaginative forms. Similarly, the faculty which replaces the senses is not reason, as ordinarily understood, but the mysterious faculty which in the *Prelude* Wordsworth calls 'Spiritual Love' or 'Imagination'.

His rather diffuse attempts in the *Prelude* to explain the nature of this faculty are not entirely satisfactory. We may perhaps achieve an approach to his meaning if we carry our minds back for a brief space to a peculiarly Wordsworthian doctrine of which something has already been said. ' Poetry has its origin ', Wordsworth says, in the preface to *Lyrical Ballads*, ' in emotion recollected in tranquillity.' In connexion with this doctrine I have called attention to Wordsworth's own method of poetical composition. The poem, with him, always follows the emotion, or incident, which it describes at a very respectful distance, at an interval, often, of as much as ten years. He was persuaded (and, no doubt, in his case it was the fact) that the essential truth of a given emotion, or incident, came thus to be more completely expressed. In this doctrine, as in everything else, he starts out from his own experience. That was how he himself made into poetry the emotions and incidents given to him by nature and the senses. In what exactly the process of making into poetry all this raw material offered by the senses consists, is another question. At the moment, and for our present purpose, it does not particularly matter. What matters is the inference drawn by Wordsworth from what he finds to happen. If the truth of an emotion can be best expressed in a season of tranquillity, even ten or twenty years after

Sense and Imagination

it was experienced, it will be consonant with this that the glory of the natural world should continue to work in us, and we to work upon it, years after the visionary gleams of sense have ceased to illuminate our daily walk.

With this clue in our minds, let us return to the great *Ode*. In lines 193-5 of that poem,

> Think not of any severing of our loves,

Wordsworth says to the hills and woods and streams;

> Yet in my heart of hearts I feel your might.
> I only have relinquished one delight
> To live beneath your more habitual sway.

Here, even the innocent phrase 'heart of hearts' is not without its significance. Elsewhere Wordsworth speaks of the 'heart within the heart' (*Excursion*, iv. 629): using the expression to denote that part of our nature which apprehends 'the light of truth' without employing either the senses or the scientific reason. It is this faculty of which he speaks, then, in line 193. 'Heart of hearts' means the imagination as distinguished from (*a*) the senses and (*b*) reason.

The meaning of lines 194-5 has been endlessly debated. I accept, in the main, the interpretation offered by Mr. Gordon Wordsworth,[1] the poet's grandson: 'I have relinquished one delight, i.e. the glory and the dream— only with the result that I am living under nature's more habitual sway.' So far, I think the interpretation is right. But Mr. Gordon Wordsworth amplifies further: '(I have) exchanged the spontaneous intuitive response to nature for a conscious and voluntary submission.'

[1] Cited by Mr. Harper, ii, p. 127, note. To the same effect Mr. E. H. Coleridge and Miss Arnold.

No, I think not. I think the key to the words ' habitual sway ' must be sought in Wordsworth's use of ' habitual ' elsewhere. ' Habitual ' means with him elsewhere that which is knit to, and bound up with, the affections. An illuminating passage in this connexion is *Prelude*, i. 597–612 :

> And if the vulgar joy by its own weight
> Wearied itself out of the memory,
> The scenes which were a witness of that joy
> Remained in their substantial lineaments
> Depicted on the brain, and to the eye
> Were visible, a daily sight ; and thus
> By the impressive discipline of fear,
> By pleasure and repeated happiness,
> So frequently repeated, and by force
> Of obscure feelings representative
> Of things forgotten, these same scenes so bright,
> So beautiful, so majestic in themselves,
> Though yet the day was distant, did become
> *Habitually dear*, and all their forms
> And changeful colours by invisible links
> Were *fastened to the affections*.

The glory of the senses passes into a glory of the imagination precisely by being ' fastened to the affections '.[1] That is why in the fourteenth book of the *Prelude* Imagination is identified with ' Spiritual Love ' (and Intellectual Love). Lines 188–205 of that book are of first-rate importance. Wordsworth has been speaking of the beauty of Nature, in its widest sense, as seen first in the fields, then in the beasts of the field and their

---

[1] In passing I would ask the reader to notice that in lines 601–3 Wordsworth says that the memories of which he is speaking remained with him for a long period, not merely ' depicted on the brain ', but as actual visual images (' to the eye were visible, a daily sight '); and once again, I think that he means what he says—and that we have to reckon with a faculty distinctively abnormal.

Sense and Imagination

dumb affections, and finally in what he calls 'the earth-born passions of men', i.e. the love that is of the senses. These achieve value only in so far as they are quickened by 'Spiritual Love', and pass into the imagination:

> This Spiritual Love acts not nor can exist
> Without Imagination, which, in truth,
> Is but another name for absolute power,
> And clearest insight, amplitude of mind,
> And Reason in her most exalted mood.
> This faculty hath been the feeding source
> Of our long labour; we have traced the stream
> From the blind cavern whence is faintly heard
> Its natal murmur; followed it to light
> And open day; accompanied its course
> Among the works of nature; for a time [1]
> Lost sight of it bewildered and engulphed;
> Then given it greeting as it rose once more
> In strength, reflecting from its placid breast
> The works of man and face of human life;
> And lastly from its progress have we drawn
> Faith in life endless, the sustaining thought
> Of human being, eternity and God.

It will be noticed here that the imaginative faculty is called 'Reason in her most exalted mood'. That is to say, it is a higher reason than mere reason—and indeed a quite separate faculty. With the scientific reason, which Wordsworth consistently attacks (even in his later period he attacks it) it has nothing at all to do. The imaginative faculty is that faculty which, by binding the things of sense to the moral affections, transmutes them, makes them a part of poetry—whether the poetry of books or of life—and, in so doing, links us with the things in the world which are permanent, and

[1] The Godwinian period.

assures us of immortality. The vision of the senses melts and dissolves, but it melts into the revelation of permanent supersensual realities. The fashion of the world passes away; but it fades before a mind conscious of an order of things fashioned immortally.

It will be noticed further that, in the passage quoted, Wordsworth speaks of having, in the *Prelude*, traced the stream of the imagination

> From the blind cavern where is faintly heard
> Its natal murmur.

I said before that his sensationalism was not mere sensationalism, for the reason that sense, in its highest and purest activity, outran itself. In every impression of sense Wordsworth conceives that there is present *from the beginning* an imaginative activity. Sense and imagination are two extremes in the scale of poetic, or spiritual, apprehension: but the higher faculty is always obscurely present in the lower. In our perception of Nature there is always (*a*) a sense-impression given from without, and (*b*) an activity of the mind, a contribution, however inchoate in form, from the imagination; or, if there is not, then neither is Nature seen in its beauty nor Man in his proper grandeur. But this contribution of the imagination means that we ourselves to some extent create Nature. And in more than one passage of Wordsworth this doctrine is pretty directly announced. It appears, fully formulated, in a passage of the *Recluse* which, from letters of Wordsworth himself, we know to have been written before 1804.[1] Wordsworth says that he will proclaim how exquisitely the mind is

---

[1] See Grosart, ii, pp. 163–5, and the letter cited by Mr. Harper, in vol. ii, p. 80.

Sense and Imagination

fitted to the external world and the external world to the mind, and will expound

> the creation (by no lower name
> Can it be called) which they with blended might
> Accomplish.

Similarly, in a passage of the *Prelude*, which we have already had occasion to notice, he tells us that, even in the visionary experiences of his childhood 'an auxiliar might came from his mind' bestowing 'new splendour' on the forms of Nature (ii. 359-70). This 'auxiliar might' he calls a 'creative sensibility' (ii. 360); and in *Tintern Abbey*, it will be recalled, he speaks of the 'mighty world' which 'eye and ear' half create and half perceive. In all these passages he is groping his way—obscurely, I think, and confusedly—towards a philosophy of the interrelation of the senses and imagination. With this his mind was undoubtedly occupied while he was composing the great *Ode*. The ultimate source of the doctrine which he sought to adumbrate is, of course, the writings of those German philosophers whose opinions so powerfully influenced Coleridge. And the influence of Coleridge at the time of the composition of the *Ode* may be seen clearly by comparison of one of Coleridge's poems—a poem written just when Wordsworth was beginning the *Ode*, and addressed to Wordsworth—I mean the poem *Dejection*. An external bond between the two compositions is perhaps indicated by the fact that Wordsworth's first stanza begins with the same five words as Coleridge's sixth—'There was a time when...'[1] It is worth while

[1] But the words occur, at the beginning of a line, in *The Mad Monk* (written 1800). Wordsworth's first stanza was undoubtedly written with some reminiscence of lines 9-12 of *The Mad Monk*.

to set out here the third, fourth, and fifth stanzas of Coleridge's poem:

My genial spirits fail;
But what can these avail
To lift the smothering weight from off my breast?
It were a vain endeavour,
Though I should gaze for ever
On that green light that lingers in the west:
I may not hope from outward forms to win
The passion and the life, whose fountains are within.

O William, we receive but what we give,
And in our life alone doth Nature live:
Ours is her wedding garment, ours her shroud.
And would we aught behold of higher worth,
Than that inanimate cold world allowed
To the poor loveless over-anxious crowd,
Ah! from the soul itself must issue forth
A light, a glory, a fair luminous cloud
Enveloping the earth—
And from the soul itself must there be sent
A sweet and potent voice, of its own birth,
Of all sweet sounds the life and element!

O pure of heart! *thou* needst not ask of *me*
What this strong music in the soul may be!
What, and wherein it doth exist,
This light, this glory, this fair luminous mist,
This beautiful and beauty-making power.
Joy, blameless poet, Joy that ne'er was given,
Save to the pure, and in their purest hour,
Life and Life's effluence, cloud at once and shower,
Joy, William, is the spirit and the power,
Which, wedding Nature to us,[1] gives in dower
A new Earth and new Heaven,

---

[1] In the editions the line appears (twice) with a false punctuation, seriously vitiating the sense. Joy is the spirit which weds Nature to us, and, in so doing, gives us a new earth and heaven.

Undreamt of by the sensual and the proud:
Joy is the sweet voice, Joy the luminous cloud—
We in ourselves rejoice !
And thence flows all that charms or ear or sight,
All melodies the echo of that voice,
All colours a suffusion from that light

Coleridge there, as will have been observed, goes a good deal beyond Wordsworth; he throws all the emphasis upon the creative faculty of the imagination, and seems wholly to eliminate, as a source of any pure joy, the activity of the senses. Wordsworth never, in any period, advances so far as that; and indeed, it is difficult to see how he could have done so without abandoning completely the greater part of his metaphysical sensationalism. But the ideas which Coleridge here turns to such bold and splendid effects (effects, it must be confessed, in their own *genus*, beyond Wordsworth's powers) were obviously, at the time when he wrote the *Ode* upon Immortality, a good deal exercising Wordsworth's mind—and, I think, not a little perplexing it. ' *Thou* needst not ask of *me* ', says Coleridge. But I am not sure that there was not need. It is far from easy to apprehend the nature of the answer which Wordsworth at this very time was dimly endeavouring to formulate to the question which the *Ode* raises. When eyes and ears, in which we have put our trust, cease to give us vision and the sound of the world, what have we to fall back upon ? Wordsworth's answer is, as I understand him, not simply that we are living upon past memories—incorrigible improvidents subsisting upon our spiritual capital—but that, if we have connected the glory of sense, while it stayed, with the affections, with the moral element in our nature:

then, the decay of sense, the passing of the old gift of seeing, yet leaves us rich in the only true riches, the activity of the imagination. The images of sense with which we have stored our spirit do not lie in it, or upon it, inert and motionless, without warmth or colour. The activity of the imagination not only keeps alive past images, but it is constantly bringing to birth, and calling into truth, images which, when they were first presented to us, failed of their effect, or, because mixed with much that was unessential, hit only a partial effect. But the material which the senses have furnished is almost infinite; and the imagination is kept endlessly employed. Perpetually, it works in tranquillity—in what Wordsworth, in the *Ode*, calls 'a season of calm weather'—it works in genuine creative fashion upon emotions and impressions often infinitely remote; and from its working there proceeds that 'principle of joy' which makes good life and good poetry.

All this the *Ode* does not say; and even when we have supplemented it from the *Prelude* and from such other work of Wordsworth's great period as is relevant, we stop far short of a fully reasoned doctrine of the imaginative life. Perhaps, indeed, in the *Ode*, Wordsworth has not done more than indicate, and emphasize, what he conceives to be the principal element, or source, of the imaginative, or creative faculty—the element which consists in binding the beauty given by the senses to the affections, to the moral part of our nature. That at any rate is the note upon which the poem ends:

> Thanks to the human heart by which we live,
> Thanks to its tenderness, its joys, and fears,
> To me the meanest flower that blows can give
> Thoughts that do often lie too deep for tears.

And in his later work, it is when he is able to strike again from time to time the same note, clearly and sweetly, that he makes his tenderest appeal. Here are some verses, written, it is believed, as late as 1845, in which we may still catch something of the accent of his supreme period:

> Glad sight whenever new with old
> Is joined through some dear home-born tie;
> The life of all that we behold
> Depends upon that mystery.
>
> Vain is the glory of the sky,
> The beauty vain of field and grove,
> Unless, while with admiring eye
> We gaze, we also learn to love.

X

'THE WATERS SLEEP'

COLERIDGE speaks of himself somewhere as flowing into the stream of Wordsworth's genius 'in a hundred nameless rills'. About the time that the great *Ode* was finished there began that breach between himself and Wordsworth which, while it was to some extent patched up, was never truly healed. From about 1806 Coleridge in fact ceased to be a direct formative influence in Wordsworth's life and thought. From the same period dates that decline in Wordsworth's poetical powers which no obtuseness can miss and no ingenuity satisfactorily explain. A factor in it, I have suggested, may have been an essential abnormality of faculty. The postulate of the sudden and early decay of a faculty of vision abnormally developed and abnormally exercised is, perhaps, not in itself absurd. It must be admitted, however, that it carries us into realms of speculation where we may be chargeable, not unfairly, with illuminating one darkness by another. The operations of genius are, in all examples of it, mysterious ; and it is possible that most of our mistakes about it proceed from our failure to realize the degree to which this (which we all admit in words) is true : from a failure in us to assent effectively to the truism that inspired men belong to a different order from that of ordinary men. The odd turns of inspiration never fail to find us surprised and protesting ; and when we have used ourselves to a genius which (like most genius) is inspired on and off over a long period of years, we let ourselves be taken unawares by a genius consistently inspired for ten years on end, and then, for fifty, continuously uninspired.

Be this as it may, it is certain that the estrangement of Wordsworth from Coleridge could not have happened at a season more unfortunate in its consequences to the talents of the former. The persuasion that Wordsworth was ordained to the destiny of being a great philosophic poet was one which Wordsworth himself did not entertain more fervently than his friend. With that gift which he had for enabling others to those great undertakings from which by a constitutional infirmity of will he was himself perpetually inhibited, Coleridge had placed Wordsworth's feet in the path of philosophy; and in 1807 Wordsworth would have seemed to be advancing in a sure and straight course. But no sooner is Coleridge withdrawn, than he not merely falters in an unfinished work, he not merely stops, he turns back. It was enough that he should do no more. But he undoes what he has done. One of Wordsworth's slighter, and less-known poems, has for its theme the estrangement from Coleridge—such at any rate is the usual interpretation; and it is not easy to see that the piece is susceptible of any other. It is entitled the *Complaint*, and, written in 1806, was published in 1807:

> There is a change—and I am poor
> Your love hath been, nor long ago,
> A fountain at my fond heart's door,
> Whose only business was to flow;
> And flow it did; not taking heed
> Of its own bounty, or my need.[1]

[1] The coincidence between lines 3-6 and Coleridge's remark, cited above, that he flowed into the stream of Wordsworth's genius 'in a hundred nameless rills', is not a little notable.

> What happy moments did I count!
> Blest was I then all bliss above!
> Now, for that consecrated fount
> Of murmuring, sparkling, living love,
> What have I? Shall I dare to tell?
> A comfortless and hidden well.
>
> A well of love—it may be deep—
> I trust it is—and never dry:
> What matter? if the waters sleep
> In silence and obscurity.
> —Such change, and at the very door
> Of my fond heart, hath made me poor.

'There is a change, and I am poor'. The words are truer than Wordsworth meant them to be, or at any rate, far wider in their application. He is speaking of the affections. But he is poorer, not only in the wealth of the affections, but in the riches of philosophic thought; and there lie before him more than forty years of this philosophic and poetic poverty—a long period illuminated now and again by flashes of the old vision, but in the main lamentably dull and drab, the most dismal anti-climax of which the history of literature holds record.

No one who has followed with any attention what has already been said of the metaphysical theories which lie behind Wordsworth's poetry will have failed to perceive in connexion with these a great deal that is left inchoate and, indeed, confused. In particular, in respect of the relation of the imagination to the logical reason many, or rather most, of the questions that present themselves remain undetermined. The two powers confront one another in a sort of armed neutrality. With the forces of the imagination are leagued those of the senses; but as between the forms given to the senses and those rendered back by the imagination, it is not always easy to divine which are the shadows and which the substance. I have the feeling that amid the philosophic doubts which Wordsworth had thus raised for himself, and us, he stood, in 1807, in a situation more perplexed than either his pride could allow or his unaided reflections expedite. Perhaps only Coleridge could have helped him—Coleridge with his careless gift (to no one more acceptable than to Wordsworth) of bestowing benefits with the fine air of a man who receives them. Coleridge was, in any case, one of those minds which startle other minds out of the *ordinariness* which so easily besets most men, and besets at fitful intervals even genius. We have noticed already how Wordsworth was conscious of, and even emphasizes the presence of, a certain ordinariness in his own nature and habits. He saw himself as in general a very boyish boy, and again as a very average undergraduate, and yet again as a youth like so many others, vacillating between rebellion and listlessness. Yet he beheld always, as it were, a silver thread of 'vision' variegating this ordinariness, in all periods of its manifestation. Coleridge also saw the ordinariness. He lamented in Wordsworth, says Hazlitt, 'a something corporeal, a matter-of-factness, a clinging to the palpable'. Nor did it, as we all know, escape the observation of De Quincey, who so often, in his account of Wordsworth, replaces the poet by the shrewd and hard-headed and somewhat contentious Dalesman. Coleridge, as I say, was one of those men in whose presence it is difficult to be ordinary. He had (with whatever faults) that generosity of temper which rouses others to their proper greatness—the mere sound of his voice was, as Hazlitt says, ' the music of thought '. The withdrawal of his influence carried with it, for Wordsworth, not only, as I think, philosophical impoverishment, but a kind of relapse into ordinariness. From 1807 on, Wordsworth sinks deeper and deeper into ordinariness—like a man relapsing into some sensual indulgence ; he drugs himself with the humdrum of political and social and religious orthodoxy ; and only now and again, in some mysteriously appointed casual re-awakening, does he shake off the influence—else ever intensifying—of the deadly opiate.

If these seem depressing reflections, yet they have this much in them that is re-fortifying : that of a world, where so much proceeds by rule of thumb, one of the facts, none the less, is the being of genius ; of which the principal character is its dominant unpredictability. Those who believe in it, who believe that there really and truly is an order of inspired men, having qualities actually different in kind from those of other men, have small reason to be either surprised or affronted as they mark in poets the odd comings and goings of their greatness and dullness. It is no little thing, after all, if over a period of ten years we can detain an unintermitted fullness of inspired being.

The reader was admonished betimes that he was not to look in these pages for that display of the arts of literary appreciation which is elsewhere only too freely current. Yet I would not have it supposed that any man could close his reading of Wordsworth upon a note of negation or disparagement or reserve. Of the mightier passions which shake the soul and rock the world, of man's wrath and love and jealousy, other poets are the more animated artists. Of the lights and shades of human character other poets have expressed a subtler or more telling image. And of the great actions in which character and passion are summed, and which are, when all is said and done, the proper object of the supreme poets, others give us more fully the motion and meaning. Nor, again, can I think that Wordsworth is, as he certainly aspired to be, a great philosophic poet. None the less, in his best poetry, in the poetry of his supreme decade, he has left to us work of a unique quality; work which supplies a more powerful aid to the imaginative life than is secured to us in the poetry of far greater poets. It is not difficult to feel the sway of great actions and passions as Shakespeare gives them life for us; nor perhaps, to submit our souls to the solemn religious harmonies of Milton, to subdue ourselves to that immitigable grandeur. But among the commonplaces of life, environed by custom and the casual cares of the world, still to live imaginatively—this is not easy, and this, more than other poets, Wordsworth helps us to do. He brings to us, as no one else does, images and intuitions which light the common face of life, throwing into new, and truer, relations the parts of that great, but confused, order of things which is Nature. And these images and intuitions he clothes in a language which, if it is sometimes mean, is never meretricious; a language the bare truthfulness of which not only attests the purity of thought and intention from which itself proceeds, but supplies, as it were, a pattern by which, in the speech of other men—whether in poetry or in prose or in the common uses of conversation—we can appraise what there is of reality and strength. No one, I could fancy, who has once felt deeply the influence of Wordsworth's mind and style, will be easily deceived—he will certainly be less easily deceived than other men—by what, whether in the world or in the mind or in literary style, is *showy*.[1] It is the condition of a developed culture, and of complex social relations, that they tend to enslave us to modes of thought and feeling and expression that are factitious. As a force liberating us from the perils of this condition no poetry, perhaps, operates more powerfully and benignly than that of Wordsworth; for no other poetry so insistently and successfully recalls us to those elements of nature upon which the imaginative life depends.

[1] More readily, perhaps, in Wordsworth than anywhere else the student of poetry may acquire what Coleridge tells us that he learned from the German poet, Opitz: 'a sort of tact for what is genuine in the style of later writers' (*Biogr. Lit.*, chap. x).

xi
THE PREFACE TO 'LYRICAL BALLADS'

THE work of Wordsworth's effective period is consciously dominated (as the pages preceding have, I may hope, sufficiently indicated) by what may be called his metaphysic of the imagination. This domination makes itself felt the more insistently, perhaps, for the very reason that its credentials are not complete and in order. It is characteristic, doubtless, of all greatness that it raises (for itself, as well as for us) more questions than it can answer; and at least as early as 1800 Wordsworth had entered a path of philosophic speculation where (as I have already suggested) he moved among embarrassments of which he was sometimes almost painfully conscious. Losing touch, about the year 1807, with Coleridge (being divorced at any rate from that intimate communion with him which had both originated and sustained his metaphysical interests), he drifted gradually into a disposition in which he was content to leave undetermined much of the outline of his philosophy of poetry. When all is said and done, his theory of the interaction of sense and imagination hangs in air. I have called him a sensationalist; and much of his earliest, and best, poetry breathes an almost unqualified sensationalism. And to the unspoiled senses he still looks for truth, even in that portion of his work which belongs to his late and dull period. He carries into old age the crusade against intellectualism—if his arm flags, he still bears in his heart something of the old crusading spirit. On the other hand, it is clear from many parts of the *Prelude*, and they are early, that the material of the poetic imagination, though it is sense-material, and though it is 'passion', is conceived as undergoing, before it passes, or can pass, into poetry, some species of refining process. It is in his failure to define with any closeness the nature of this process that Wordsworth's metaphysic is principally defective; and, perhaps not all which he says upon the subject is consistent with itself. Certainly the process is in no sort an intellectualizing one. The path from sense to imagination, from nature to poetry, does not pass through the intellect. It passes through the affections. Of the origin of the affections, the primary moral notions, and of the precise fashion in which they are enabled to mediate between sense and imagination, Wordsworth tells us either nothing or nothing that is coherent. There are passages in the *Prelude*, where, as we have already seen, Wordsworth plainly intimates that in all sense-perception there is an element which is not mere sense. This intrusive element is what I may call the *affectual* part of our nature; but by what laws it inheres in (and moralizes) the whole context, and each detail, of our sensuous experience, we are never plainly told. But only as it does so are we able to pass from the perception of nature to the imaging, or imagining, of it; to convert the splendour of the world of sense into the glory of poetry.

Much of this, as I say, hangs in air. But we shall not understand either Wordsworth's practice in poetry or the literary theory with which that practice connects unless we bear in mind that both are founded in this inchoate metaphysic. Out of this metaphysic proceed

The Preface to 'Lyrical Ballads'

both the *Lyrical Ballads* and the Preface to the *Lyrical Ballads*.

The Preface appeared first in 1800,[1] replacing the short *Advertisement* which had been prefixed to the edition of 1798. It belongs, accordingly to a period of Wordsworth's life in which his imagination was especially vigorous, and his courage and temper unimpaired. The style, if in the main it studies nobility rather than convenience,[2] is none the less of a character easily justifying the sweeping assertion of his old age—that 'all great poets write good prose . . . there is not one

[1] It was written, for the most part, in September of 1800, with an addition made in October (*Journals of Dorothy Wordsworth*, i, pp. 49, 50, 52). In 1802 there was added to it the Appendix, on Poetic Diction, and in the text of it there was incorporated a passage of some eighteen pages (pp. 56-64 in Knight's edition), containing the justly famous delineation of the character of the poet, and developing the contrast between that character and the qualities which belong to the man of science. In the poems of 1815 the preface to *Lyrical Ballads* is printed in an appendix, and the collection has a new preface of its own accompanied by an Essay Supplementary. (The essay is supplementary, not, as the editions of Lord Morley and Mr. Hutchinson might suggest, to the Preface of 1800, but to that of 1815.) The new preface is academically conceived and phrased, and it is not always easy to reconcile it with the preface of 1800. It contains the famous, but useless, distinction (foreshadowed in a note to the *Thorn*, 1800) between the imagination and the fancy; and one paragraph of fine Miltonic egotism. The *Essay Supplementary* is a far worthier companion to the preface of 1800. But the earlier part of it is marred by uneasy reflections on the relation of poetry to religious orthodoxy; the middle part, which is historical, exhibits a licence of paradox quite without example, and the conclusion of it is big (or small) with self-assertion.

[2] Wordsworth might have said of his own prose what Coleridge says of his: 'An aversion to the epigrammatic unconnected periods of the fashionable Anglo-gallican taste has too often made me willing to forget that the stately march and difficult evolutions which characterize the eloquence of Hooker, Bacon, Milton, and Jeremy Taylor are, notwithstanding their intrinsic excellence, still less suited to a periodical essay' (*The Friend*, Essay iii).

exception'.[1] How indeed could it be otherwise, if there be any truth in that paradox of the Preface by which it is most remembered—'there neither is nor can be any essential difference between the language of prose and metrical composition'?

However, the Preface was not written either to parade a flair for Miltonic prose or to defend a paradox. Paradox, in any case, is relative to its provocation; and it is at least a less paradox to call poetry prose than to have called Pope poetry. No doubt the Preface suffers here and there from a habit of faulty emphasis. That is true of most pamphlets; and the Preface to *Lyrical Ballads* (though it is much besides) *is* a piece of pamphleteering. It is, indeed, first-class pamphleteering; that is to say, it does what it starts to do, it kills its quarry. It is still read and talked of (to which most pamphlets neither aspire nor reach); yet perhaps that feature of it is least remembered which most deserves remembrance—its immediate and enduring effectiveness. It will be, as long as we are interested in our own poetry, an historical document of abiding importance; not so much, it is likely, for what it brings of true theory, as for what it abolished of false practice. Coleridge was averse from the publication of the Preface; and many years later he expressed the opinion that it had acted unfavourably to the appreciation of Wordsworth's poetry. With this judgement I suppose Wordsworth himself must have concurred when he wrote, in 1815, that 'it was not an agreeable office, *nor a prudent undertaking*, to declare' the opinions expressed in the Preface. Yet there is, I think, reason for believing that upon the direction of public taste the Preface, exciting not only

[1] *Reminiscences of Lady Richardson*, Grosart, iii, p. 453.

curiosity, but 'in many cases' (as Coleridge says) 'acrimonious passions', exercised an immediate influence far in excess of what the *Lyrical Ballads* themselves could have achieved. The first edition of *Lyrical Ballads* (without the Preface) failed to arrest any serious degree of interest. It did little more than set a puzzle to the solution of which the *Advertisement* furnished only an inadequate key. It was difficult for the casual student of poetry to discover what his author would be at. And there was a good deal to offend him. The truth is that the *Ballads* are, in many examples, more provocative than the Preface. The Preface was a keen north wind, blowing with unmistakable power upon inveterated opinion; and far more easily understood than the eerie, even crazy, whistlings of some of the *Ballads*. The Preface sent the *Lyrical Ballads* almost at once into a third edition, provoking at the same time an American edition (and comment in the American journals). In 1805 a fourth edition was called for.

Not all the Preface, of course, was understood; in particular not the metaphysical presuppositions which lie behind it [1]—or even that there were any. It was taken at its face value; and that a high one: as a protest, conceived in a spirit somewhat extreme, against that conventional diction, called poetic, which, as we now recognize, does in fact deprive much that in the verse of the eighteenth century is genuinely poetry of the title to be called by that name. So taken, it had practical workings swifter, and more immediate, than is commonly realized. Fifteen years later, Wordsworth

[1] The *British Critic* (1801, p. 125) speaks already of the Preface as 'written in some parts with a degree of metaphysical obscurity'.

is able already, in the *Essay Supplementary*, to employ, in respect of the canons of literary criticism which had dominated literature throughout the period separating Milton from Thomson, language in which these canons are marked as finally discredited. The Preface to *Lyrical Ballads*, or the decade of reflection following it, extinguished for good and all the repute of standards to which 'that distinguished event' (as Wordsworth calls it), the publication of the *Lives of the Poets*, had seemed to give immortal currency. Most of the credit for this Wordsworth assigns, it is true, to the *Lyrical Ballads* themselves: unconscious, as always, that the inextricable confusion, in those pieces, of good and bad practice had done almost as much to cloud as to clear contemporary judgement. Such element of paradox as the Preface contained was at least vivifying. But the practical paradox of the *Ballads* was depressing.

Of the *Lyrical Ballads* in their first edition, it is worth observing: first, that there is but one ballad among them, and that this, as its title, and the orthography of its title, sufficiently indicate, does not at all conform to the description of the purpose of the Collection which the *Advertisement* offers—'an experiment to ascertain how far the language of conversation in the middle and lower classes of society is adapted to the purposes of poetic pleasure'; [1] and secondly, that those parts of the Collection which can rank as great or decisive are precisely those which make no pretence to be lyrical. Wordsworth's three poems [2] in blank verse plainly

[1] Dr. Burney, who reviewed *Lyrical Ballads* in the *Monthly Review*, 1799, xxix, pp. 202 sqq., criticizes the author's zeal 'to give artificial rust to modern poetry'.

[2] *Lines Left upon a Seat in a Yew-tree, Old Man travelling, Tintern Abbey*.

The Preface to 'Lyrical Ballads'

touch greatness; and the same is true of the three [1] contributed by Coleridge. The *Female Vagrant*, again, is, if not great, decisive—decisive for new opportunities of style. Among the lyrics two,[2] certainly, are supreme in their kind, and that a new kind; and two others [3] are at least fresh and charming. Of the rest of the book [4] it is best to say plainly that Wordsworth might have gone on writing like it for a half-century and more —and to-day not rank with the great poets. The truth is that those poems in the book which attempt the 'experiment' announced in the *Advertisement* fail. The experiment in itself was, it should be allowed, a perfectly legitimate one—to discover whether poetry can be written in the language of conversation, as that is employed by persons in a humble situation of society. In such a language, beyond a doubt, poetry has been written; but by few poets (oddly enough) with so little success as by Wordsworth himself.[5]

Of this he was himself, it may be suspected, in 1800, not altogether unconscious. I infer this, firstly, from the fact that he suppressed for more than twenty years his

[1] *The Foster-Mother's Tale, The Nightingale, The Dungeon.*

[2] 'It is the first mild day of March,' and *Lines Written in Early Spring*.

[3] *Expostulation and Reply, The Tables Turned.*

[4] Which includes, it must be allowed, *Simon Lee, We are Seven*, and the *Anecdote for Fathers*, pieces which I should describe as attracting, but not compelling.

[5] I except in saying this a piece which Wordsworth himself never printed, *The Tinker* (written in 1802). Portions of it are bungled; but much of it has what most of Wordsworth's attempts in this sort lack, a genuine Shakesperian gusto. Nothing could be better than its opening lines:

> Who leads a happy life
> If it's not the merry Tinker?
> Not too old to have a wife,
> Not too much a thinker.

The whole may be seen in Mr. Nowell Smith's edition, iii, p. 423.

LYRICAL BALLADS,

WITH

A FEW OTHER POEMS.

LONDON:
PRINTED FOR J. & A. ARCH, GRACECHURCH-STREET.
1798.

The Preface to 'Lyrical Ballads'

most considerable venture in this style, *Peter Bell*; and secondly, from the fact that, while the *Lyrical Ballads* of 1800 include one or two short pieces in the early bad manner, in general they break from it decisively: their strength is that of the volume of 1798—firstly, blank verse (*Michael, The Brothers*, 'There was a boy . . .'), and secondly, the pure lyrical strain of such unmatched work as the Lucy poems, the *Fountain*, the *Two April Mornings*, the *Poet's Epitaph*. But yet more informing is the Preface. No word more does the Preface say about an experiment ' to ascertain how far the language of conversation in the lower and middle class is adapted to the purposes of poetic pleasure '. Instead, we hear of ' an experiment . . . to ascertain how far, by fitting to metrical arrangement a selection of the language of men in a state of vivid sensation, that sort of pleasure and that quantity of pleasure may be imparted which a poet may rationally endeavour to impart '. Of this new formula (introduced somewhat slyly, as though its author trusted to luck that the reader had by this time forgotten the terms of the *Advertisement*), of this new formula it may fairly be said that it has had to carry a burden of comment too heavy for a paradox—or a truism: criticism has indifferently conceived it as the one and the other. Probably—as we shall see—it is nearer to truism than to paradox. But that it is neither, it owes to its connexions. These we have now to examine.

Prefixed to the second edition of *Lyrical Ballads* there stands a line of Latin verse of which the ultimate source is not traceable:[1]

Quam nihil ad genium, Papiniane, tuum!

[1] Coleridge took it from Selden's preface to the *Illustrations* of Drayton's *Polyolbion*. See Hutchinson's reprint of *Lyrical Ballads*, 1798, p. lviii. Selden perhaps made the line himself.

Absent from the first edition, this versicle (oddly wrested from whatever may have been its original application[1]) would seem to give us our first hint of what the author of the *Lyrical Ballads* is after: he will have nothing to do with that order of talent which distinguishes the 'Papinian', the hanger-on of the school of Pope. In the *Essay Supplementary* (1815) Wordsworth traces in rapid, but heavy, outline the history of English poetry and poetical taste during 'the greater part of the last two centuries'. Dr. Johnson had taught him that 'there was before the time of Dryden no poetical diction';[2] and reflection had led him to the opinion that, after Dryden, there was nothing else. That Dryden was in fact the first of the Wordsworthians, it was hardly to be expected that Wordsworth should divine. None the less, that radical reformation of the diction of English poetry which Dryden began, and which Pope completed, took its origin from ideals not dissimilar to those of the Preface to *Lyrical Ballads*. If Dryden did not always employ, yet he consistently advocated the employment, in poetry, of 'plain English'; and against his earliest poetry there was directed the same criticism as met that of Wordsworth—it 'wanted, not only height of fancy, but dignity of words to set it forth'.[3] We may suppose, indeed, that, if it had been asked of either Dryden or Pope, in what respects they conceived themselves principally to have improved the poetry of their country, either would have answered that he had laboured to supersede a conventional jargon by a diction 'near to the real language of men'; and that Pope at least would have

[1] In Selden the words mean 'how much *inferior* to your talent, Papinian'.

[2] *Lives of the Poets*, Hill, i, p. 420.

[3] *Annus Mirabilis*, Preface, *ad finem*.

pointed to the manner in which, both in his theory and in his practice, he had been at pains to commend a 'selection' of that language 'purified . . . from all lasting causes of dislike or disgust'. In such favourite phrases of Wordsworth either might properly have described his aims; and it is likely that to Dryden at any rate the *dictum* that 'there neither is nor can be any essential difference between the language of prose and metrical composition' would have appeared a good deal less paradoxical than it still seems to persons imperfectly acquainted with the history of the theory of poetry in England. Dryden had said things like it, and, in his own fashion, had endeavoured to live up to them. Unhappily, neither he nor Pope had made real to themselves, in connexion with the language of poetry, two vital considerations: first, that such language must express passion, and secondly, that it must base itself in just observation.

That what was wanting to the poetry of Pope and the 'Papinians' was 'passion' had been plainly said long ago (when to say it was a much more daring challenge to prejudice) by Joseph Warton. From the use made,[1]

---

[1] Warton is mentioned by name in the *Essay Supplementary* as the first writer to call attention to the merits of Thomson (see the *Essay upon the Genius and Writings of Pope*, section ii, vol. i, pp. 40 sqq., ed. 5, 1806). But other passages indicate that in 1815 Wordsworth was fresh from the perusal of Warton. 'It is somewhat strange', says Warton, 'that in the pastorals of a young poet, there should not be found a single rural image that is new' (i, p. 4). Of this remark the very phrases are echoed by Wordsworth in a passage of the *Essay Supplementary*, cited below, p. 169; and with it may be compared Warton's reference, i, p. 19, to 'the few images introduced in (Windsor Forest) . . . which are not equally applicable to any place whatever'. Wordsworth shares with Warton his appreciation of Dyer (see Warton, i, p. 35). Warton, ii, p. 170, speaks of 'the pleasing effect that the use of common and familiar

in the *Essay Supplementary*, of Warton's book on Pope, it has been too readily, I think, inferred that the book was known to Wordsworth when he wrote the Preface of 1800. If it was so, Wordsworth is, in the Preface, at least as much the critic as the continuator of Warton. Warton is before all the enthusiast of (what he desiderates in Pope) ' the creative and glowing imagination '.[1] So—as we shall see—is Wordsworth; but—as we shall also see—in the Preface he is not over-anxious to emphasize this. In the Preface, as it was first drafted, he is ostentatiously uninterested in what may be called the ' ecstatics ' of poetry. Throughout he looks rather at the feet than at the wings of poetry. This excessive absorption in the homely, rather than in the celestial, character of poetry, is in some degree corrected in the edition of 1802 by the interpolation, already noticed, of a long passage on ' the character of the poet '. But even here, when he tells us that ' the poet thinks and feels in the spirit of human passions ', he underscores the word *human*. It is worth observing that throughout the Preface the word ' imagination ' occurs but twice.[2] Wordsworth is far more interested in a different, and lower faculty, observation. Of the value of this faculty Warton was not unaware. But that just observation is the source of a pure diction—this he left it to Wordsworth to see and to say.

Certainly the ambition of recalling poetry to the language of prose was not among Warton's aims. More

words and objects, judiciously managed, produce(s) in poetry '; citing, in illustration, Dryden. Wordsworth neglects the illustration.

[1] Preface, p. iii.

[2] ' Poverty of language ', it is said, in the *Essay Supplementary*, ' is the primary cause of the use which we make of the word.'

The Preface to 'Lyrical Ballads'

reasonably he might be claimed as an adherent of the opinion that verse is not essential to poetry.

'Nothing can be more judicious', he says, 'than the method (Horace) prescribes, of trying whether any composition be essentially poetical or not; which is, to drop entirely the measures and numbers, and transpose and invert the order of the words : and in this unadorned manner to peruse the passage. If there be really in it a true poetical spirit, all your inversions and transpositions will not disguise and extinguish it; but it will retain its lustre, like a diamond unset, and thrown back into the rubbish of the mine. . . . Take ten lines of the Iliad, Paradise Lost, or even of the Georgics of Virgil, and see whether by any process of critical chemistry, you can lower and reduce them to the tameness of prose. You will find that they will appear like Ulysses in his disguise of rags, still a hero, though lodged in the cottage of the herdsman Eumaeus.'[1]

If, when he wrote his Preface, Wordsworth had in mind any part of Warton's work (which I am inclined to doubt), it was this passage ; and in so far as he recalls it, he is Warton's critic. A new edition of Warton's essay had appeared in 1798—it is noticed in the *Monthly Magazine* for July of that year; and the question whether metre is essential to poetry was being a good deal aired at the time in the popular literature. There can be no doubt that Wordsworth had read the discussion upon the subject in the *Monthly Magazine* carried on between *Enquirer* and *Philo-rhythmicus*.[2] The

[1] Dedication, p. vii.
[2] This has been placed beyond doubt by Miss Barstow, *Wordsworth's Theory of Poetic Diction*, p. 120 (where, however, the letter of *Philo-rhythmicus* is not noticed). The discussion begins in 1796 : *Monthly Magazine*, ii, pp. 453 sqq., and 532 sqq. Miss Barstow's suggestion that *Enquirer* is Coleridge has, I think, no probability. Her book has, however, been helpful to me here and at other points

Preface is, in fact, quite as much a defence of the employment of metre in poetry as a protest against the use of 'poetic diction'. This is more easily seen when the Preface is read in the first edition. Its opening paragraphs deal with the subject of 'what is usually called poetic diction', and throw magnificently to the winds an ornament of poetry sanctified by the practice of two centuries. Thereafter Wordsworth feels it necessary to forestall a fairly obvious objection. He has to explain why, having discarded this ornament, he yet retains the ornament of metre. If he employs in poetry the *diction* of prose (which is what, with reservations, he plainly professes let his practice be what it may), why not employ also the *numbers* of prose, rhythmical motions which creep and not soar? The direct answer to this quite pertinent question is, in the texts of the later editions, delayed by the interpolation of ten paragraphs containing 'the character of the Poet'. After this interpolation, 'It will now be proper', Wordsworth says, 'to answer an obvious question, Why, professing these opinions, have I written in verse?' He has in fact already posed the question, and in part excused himself by alleging that, whereas 'poetic diction' is lawless, metre does at least obey definite laws. He now proceeds to urge, further, that a certain 'charm' is 'by the consent of all nations' acknowledged to exist in metrical language—it is open, of course, to the captious reader to allege that among all polite peoples a like 'charm' is apprehended from 'poetic diction'. Having said this, he develops, rather obscurely, a doctrine of his own as to the manner in which metre affects the emotions. 'The end of poetry', he says, 'is to produce excitement in coexistence with an overbalance of pleasure'. The overbalance of pleasure, however, is liable to be destroyed if the excitement 'be carried beyond its proper bounds'. It is the function of metre, or it is among its functions, to 'temper and restrain the passion' of which poetry is an effect, and to 'throw a sort of half-consciousness of unsubstantial existence over the whole composition'. Thus it is that 'more pathetic situations and sentiments... may be endured in metrical composition ... than in prose.' Richardson draws tears from us, but Shakespeare never.[1]

So much having been said, Wordsworth proceeds to summarize, and to amplify, it in a paragraph of rather ambitious philosophizing:

'I have said that poetry is the spontaneous overflow of powerful feelings: it takes its origin from emotion recollected in tranquillity: the emotion is contemplated till, by a species of reaction, the tranquillity disappears and an emotion, kindred to that which was before the subject of contemplation, is gradually produced, and does itself actually exist in the mind. In this mood successful composition generally begins, and in a mood similar to this it is carried on; but the emotion, of whatever kind, and in whatever degree, from various causes, is qualified by various pleasures, so that in describing any passions whatsoever, which are voluntarily described, the mind will, upon the whole, be in a state of enjoyment. If Nature be thus cautious to preserve in a state of enjoyment a being so employed, the Poet ought to profit by the lesson held forth to him, and ought especially to take care, that, whatever passions he communicates to his Reader, those passions, if his Reader's mind be sound and vigorous, should

[1] Is this, we may ask, because *Clarissa Harlowe* is in prose, *Lear* in metre? Or is it because it is true of the supreme artist (and of him only) that, as has been said in especial of Homer, 'his voice never trembles and his hand never shakes?'

always be accompanied by an overbalance of pleasure. Now the music of harmonious metrical language, the sense of difficulty overcome, and the blind association of pleasure which has been previously received from works of rhyme or metre of the same or similar construction, [an indistinct perception perpetually renewed of language closely resembling that of real life, and yet, in the circumstance of metre, differing from it so widely] [1] —all these imperceptibly make up a complex feeling of delight, which is of the most important use in tempering the painful feelings always found intermingled with powerful descriptions of the deeper passions. This effect is always produced in pathetic and impassioned poetry; while, in lighter compositions, the ease and gracefulness with which the Poet manages his numbers are themselves confessedly a principal source of the gratification of the Reader. All that it is *necessary* to say, however, upon this subject may be effected by affirming, what few persons will deny, that, of two descriptions, either of passions, manners, or characters, each of them equally well executed, the one in prose, and the other in verse, the verse will be read a hundred times where the prose is read once.'

It is important to remember that, in this paragraph, Wordsworth's primary object is to explain the function, and justify the employment, of metre in poetry. It was not part of his intention to develop a theory of the conditions of poetical inspiration. He has, indeed, in the first two sentences thrown to us unhewn, but impressive, fragments of a theory. But these two sentences are no more than boulders of parenthesis which the poet, in his hurried course up the steep of a quite different argument, has dislodged upon us. ' Successful composition generally begins ', he tells us, in a mood which may be regarded (he does not so describe

[1] The words in brackets are absent from the edition of 1800.

it in words) as three degrees removed from the object, or incident, which it is sought to depict. There is, first, the emotion of sense set up by the object or incident itself; secondly, the recollection, or contemplation of that emotion 'in tranquillity';[1] and thirdly, there is the emotion gradually set up 'in the mind itself', an intellectual disturbance, or excitation, 'kindred to' the first emotion, but 'from various causes' 'qualified by various pleasures', and constituting, accordingly, as the first emotion does not necessarily do, a 'state of enjoyment' (the 'various causes' and the 'various pleasures' are not indicated more specifically). The sum of the effects adumbrated is ascribed to 'Nature'— which is only to say again what is given in the *dictum* that 'poetry is the *spontaneous* overflow of powerful feelings'. 'Nature' has safeguarded for the creative artist a 'state of enjoyment' in the act of creating; and he owes it to his readers to communicate to them this 'overbalance of pleasure'. A principal means of doing so consists in the use of 'the music of harmonious metrical language'. 'Painful feeling' is 'always found intermingled with powerful descriptions of the deeper passions'; and the description of such passions is the more powerful when conveyed in 'language closely resembling that of real life'. 'Yet in the circumstance of metre' the language of poetry will 'differ so widely' from real life as to create an 'indistinct perception', to 'throw a sort of half-consciousness of unsubstantial existence over the whole composition'.

The mood of imaginative creation is enjoyment. This

---

[1] This contemplative mood is described later by the phrase 'that sane state of feeling which arises out of thought'—as though it were a sort of oasis of sanity between two moods of possession.

is equally true when the creative artist treats actions and passions which are terrible, or painful, and when he treats incidents and sensations which are innocent and blithe, or even trivial. The mood is the apex of a threefold series of faculties—sensation (or perception), contemplation (or reflection), and imagination. In the Preface the apex is said to be 'kindred to' the base. Between the sensitive and the imaginative faculties (both of them passionate in character, the middle term is a mood of 'tranquillity', of 'brooding and sleeping' upon foregone sensations. The activity, or passivity, of this middle mood has a selective power. It selects in the direction of universality—at least, the faculty which is above it deals with a material from which what is unessential and accidental has been eliminated. The process of selection, elimination, filtration—call it what we will—is commonly a slow one. That is why the poet, or at least Wordsworth himself, is but rarely able to make, as he says in the *Prelude*,

A present joy the matter of a song (*Prelude*, i, p. 47)

—still less a present sorrow. Aubrey de Vere records a conversation with Wordsworth which illustrates at once the poet's theory and his practice. Speaking of an inferior descriptive poet, '" Nature ", Wordsworth said, " with flashing eye ", " Nature does not allow an inventory to be made of her charms. He should have left his pencil behind, and gone forth in a meditative spirit; and *on a later day*, he should have embodied in verse, not all he had noted, but *what he best remembered of the scene*; and he would then have presented us *with its soul*, and *not with the mere visual aspects of it* " '.[1]

[1] *Wordsworthiana*, pp. 339. See the record of a somewhat similar conversation already quoted, p. 45.

The Preface to 'Lyrical Ballads'

Wordsworth's own practice, as it would seem, almost invariable (at least when he wrote well), was to place a wide interval between the experience of his object and its poetic delineation. Sometimes he would fetch out a memory

From hiding-places ten years deep (*Waggoner*, 212)

and create upon *that*. But if the analysis which I have offered be a true one, it will now be seen how almost indecently errant are those persons (and I think that they are the majority) who have supposed that his creation proceeds from a mood of tranquillity. No! Sensation is passionate; sinking to sleep anon, losing itself in a brooding fit; but some day or other, ten years hence, it may be, 'passioning' anew in the mysteriously quickened imagination. It is this hour of passionate reawakening which is the hour of poetry. It is necessarily, where the theme treated is painful in actuality, an hour not free of pains and distresses. Especially do these attend poetic creation when the poet works under conditions in which sense still clouds the imaginative horizon, in which the emotion is in part 'in the mind itself', but in part lingers in the inferior region. But creation, where it is healthy, carries with itself joy, or what Wordsworth calls 'an overbalance of pleasure'. Shakespeare 'enjoys' *Lear*, Milton *Lycidas*, and Wordsworth *Michael*. The 'state of enjoyment' in which creation situates them is never, doubtless, wholly pure; for perfect poetry there is not, and Homer himself groaned often as he fumbled vainly for the right words and true numbers.

Throughout the Preface, let us not forget, Wordsworth is concerned rather to state the facts of poetic creation than to attempt to explain them. He is not saying more to us than that the imagination (at least as observed in himself) does so and so; what the imagination is, he does not tell us. Some of the gradations in its processes he has, indeed, distinguished; but the essential character of these processes he has neither delineated nor pretended to delineate—he attempts this first (and with an unlucky and uninforming formality, oddly redolent of the eighteenth century) in the Preface of 1815.

No part of the Preface to *Lyrical Ballads* has been more generally criticized than that in which Wordsworth affirms that the language of poetry is 'a selection of the real language of men in a state of vivid sensation'. The criticism begins with the *Biographia Literaria*—a work upon which it is usual to-day to bestow a degree of praise which I feel always to be in excess of the book's substantial merits—there is, in fact, a tendency, I think, everywhere to rate Coleridge's criticism much more highly than it deserves and, at the same time, greatly to undervalue his poetry. Wordsworth is believed to have resented much of the criticism of himself offered in the *Biographia*; and, if this was partly vanity—in which he rarely failed—he might none the less allege with justice that some parts of Coleridge's criticism were based upon culpable misunderstanding. 'The poet', Wordsworth says, 'thinks and feels in the spirit of human passions. How then can his language differ in any material degree from that of all other men who feel vividly and see clearly?' 'In order to excite rational sympathy he must express himself', not in some hieratic tongue, but 'as other men express themselves'. Now all this is not only harmless, but tonic. There could be no better opening to Wordsworth's great and enduring work—his crusade against the unreality of 'poetic diction' as it was understood by the generation to which he addressed himself. Immediately, however, he goes on to speak of the poet as 'only selecting from the real language of men, or, which amounts to the same thing, composing accurately in the spirit of such selection'; and it has been urged that if, without the qualification introduced by the reference to a 'selection', he had said simply that the true diction of poetry was 'the real language of men' in passion, a good deal of trouble would have been saved. Certainly trouble would have been saved to Coleridge; but to a more circumspect criticism, no. Coleridge, seizing upon what is said of 'selection' (with a precipitancy of judgement which makes him forget that even Johnson had used language not dissimilar), exclaims at once that a language which has submitted to this selective process will, in the result, 'not differ from the language of any other man of common sense'. Hazlitt,[1] it will be remembered, said that Coleridge had reduced the merit of Wordsworth to this— 'that there is nothing peculiar about him, and that his poetry, so far as it is good for anything at all, is just like any other good poetry'. This, we can now see, is an understatement. Coleridge in fact drags Wordsworth to the position that 'there is nothing peculiar' about poetry. And he does this by a quite perverse misunderstanding (which, unhappily, later criticism has propagated infinitely). Wordsworth has a perfectly good answer—an answer which cries itself to us from every part of his Preface. The poet who composes in

[1] *Edinburgh Review*, 1817, p. 495; reprinted Waller-Glover, vol. x, p. 142.

a selection 'from the real language of men' escapes 'the language of any other man of common sense' in the exact degree in which he is a poet. What Wordsworth says of 'selection' is not a timorous qualification, not a sly afterthought, but something essential, not merely to his theory of poetic diction, but to his whole teaching—verse and prose—upon the subject of imaginative creation. The language of poetry must be *real*, a true and not a false language; but by the same necessity (for it is to be poetry) it must be, and will be, not the language of 'common sense', but so much of the real language of men as, if I may use such an expression, will 'make up into' imagination. There must be a selective process; but the misapprehensions of subsequent criticism have been due to the failure to ask how, and by what agency, this selective process is accomplished. Once the question is posed, the answer is obvious. Just as poetry cannot work upon the objects offered to it by sense (but they must submit to a selecting and universalizing process), so it cannot work with the language of common sense, the language offered to it by real life. The language of poetry, like the stuff of poetry, comes from the imagination. The imagination operates freely, whether upon the visualized objects which are its material, or upon the language which is its principal instrument, only after there has already operated a selecting faculty. The language of poetry is to 'the language really spoken by men' exactly as the objects which the imagination visualizes are to their correlates in the sphere of sense. In both classes the imagination renders back purified and dignified what came to it, through eye and ear, confused and ignoble. If then any one asks, Who shall make that selection of the language really spoken by men which shall equip it for the high purposes of poetry, upon what principle he shall proceed, and having what ideal standard in his mind; the answer is that it lies with that Power to do it which can, and, wherever poetry is brought to birth, does, lift the mean matter of the senses into a spiritual reality.

What I have here said of diction may assist us to understand (what is a good deal more obscure) Wordsworth's conception of the function of metre; and metre, as we shall discover, like diction, has—or is a part of—a fairly defined metaphysic. In 1800 Wordsworth was certainly not easy in conscience about his own employment of metre. This may be seen, not only from the more direct handling of the problem in the text of that year, but from the fact that, in the same year, he takes up the subject in a note added to the *Thorn*.

The poet, we have seen, employs metre, in preference to writing in prose, firstly, because there is no reason why he should not—metre being, not the licentious thing that ' poetic diction ' is, but a mode of expression serving recognized laws; secondly, because metre possesses a ' charm ' in itself—a charm attested by all cultivated races; and thirdly, because metre operates to ' temper and restrain ' the ' painful feeling ' which mixes always with such ' powerful descriptions of the deeper passions ' as are achieved by the use, in poetry, of ' language closely resembling that of real life '. That there is here difficulty and obscurity can hardly be denied. For, upon a casual reading, Wordsworth would seem to say that the poet first resolves to use the language of real life because it is more powerful than any other, and that then—as though he felt that he had gone too far, had defeated his own end (or annulled his own state) of pleasure—he endeavours to save the situation by taking refuge in metre. Certainly Wordsworth says quite plainly that it is the 'tendency of metre to divest language, in a certain degree, of its reality, and to throw a sort of half-consciousness of unsubstantial existence over the whole composition'. Do we then, in poetry, lift passion by the employment of real language merely for the purpose of presently lowering it by the use of metre?

This, clearly, is not what Wordsworth means; for it conflicts, not only with good sense (which is, in his own phrase, 'one property of all good poetry'), but with his own language elsewhere. In a note which, in the year in which the Preface was written, he added to the poem entitled *The Thorn*, he says distinctly that the purpose for which he has employed, in that poem, a 'lyrical and rapid metre' is to 'convey passion' to the reader. But to what kind of reader? To one, he tells us, 'not accustomed to sympathize' with the passions of real life as they exist in, and are expressed by, a particular type of persons; one to whom such passions can only be conveyed (here I amplify) if they are first modified by, *tempered* by, poetry. It is, in fact, not the object of the poet to convey to his readers the actual passions of real men; such passions, indeed, are not the proper material of poetic creation. It is only when the poet has 'tempered and restrained' these passions that they become communicable, that they are able to be 'conveyed'.

In other words, as we can now see, the poet by the aid (among other devices) of metre, exercises upon the passions of real life the same refining and 'selecting' power as he exercises upon the language of real life. It is not that he first uses *real* language, mechanically selected and refined, and that he then tempers this, and the passions which it embodies, by the unreality of metre; but, far rather, by imaginative processes which are contemporaneous—and indeed, a unity—he uses, naturally, spontaneously, necessarily, both a 'selected' real language and the metrical forms which help to transmute real passions. The conjunct effect of these simultaneously operating imaginative processes is to 'throw', not only over 'the whole composition', but over the spirit of the reader, that half-sense of 'unsubstantial existence' in which, in truth, poetry has its life.

It may be conceded that—though not to the extent to excuse his critics—Wordsworth has expressed parts of his Preface in language not sufficiently calculated. Almost everything that he says in it implies (to a degree which the casual reader could not be expected to divine) the whole of what he has said anywhere else; it requires to be read, that is to say, in connexion with the sum of his metaphysic of poetry, his philosophy of the imagination. There are passages of the Preface, in which, read casually, he seems to speak of the selective process which fits for poetry the passions, and the language which expresses them, as though it were, not the operation of an imagination working in the mystery of its proper twilight, but an almost mechanical business of picking this or that incident or object, taking or leaving this or that element of a fortuitous vocabulary. Yet even of the sentences which I have excerpted there are more than one where an attentive reader will see that he has guarded himself. For example: 'The poet thinks and feels', he says, '*in the spirit* of human passions'—he means, in the terms of human passions that have been spiritualized. And, again, he speaks of 'composing *in the spirit* of such selection'—the spirit alone gives life to our vocabulary.

It remains true that for some part of the misapprehensions that have accompanied the criticism of the Preface Wordsworth has to thank his own faulty expression of new ideas. Mostly his expression is faulty from a wrong distribution of emphasis. Reacting not merely against a pretentious diction, but against the sum of false parade in the poetry most admired and imitated in the time in which he wrote, he was anxious, before all else, to recall art to a sense of its human connexions. 'Poets do not write', he says, wisely and mildly, 'for poets alone, but for men.' They live by the bread of a common humanity, and not by taking in one another's 'tricks, quaintnesses, hieroglyphics, and enigmas'. 'The poet must descend from his supposed height.' That the office of the poet is prophecy, that he belongs to an order of men who are rapt, possessed, uttering more than they know, Wordsworth was as well aware as other poets who have brought into greater display that element of poetry which consists in ecstasy. But when he wrote the Preface, he was primarily concerned, and properly concerned, to emphasize the connexion between what is greatest in human nature and what is most lowly; to discover in the inferior ranges of feeling unsuspected grandeur. And this disposition has committed him at times to exaggerated forms of expression; there are occasions when he seems to come perilously near to losing hold altogether of the real and solid distinctions, which do in fact subsist, between art and nature, poetry and prose. And not only this; he has been led, further, to over-emphasize in some degree those parts of the activity of the poet which are summed in ' observation '.

I have suggested already that no parts of the Preface are more valuable than those which reveal, or hint, the dependence of a pure diction upon true observation. The language of poetry is an element not dissociable, save in critical abstraction, from the matter of poetry. The intimate connexion of the two elements is clearly put to us by more than one passage of the Preface of 1800–2. But I will begin from a sentence of the *Essay Supplementary*:

' Excepting a passage or two in the *Windsor Forest* of Pope, and some delightful pictures in the Poems of Lady Winchelsea, the poetry of the period intervening between the publication of the *Paradise Lost* and *The Seasons* does not contain a single new image of external nature, and scarcely presents a familiar one from which it can be inferred that the eye of the poet had been steadily fixed upon his object, much less that his feelings had urged him to work upon it in the spirit of genuine imagination.'

In a similar spirit Wordsworth wrote to Scott about Dryden: ' That his cannot be the language of the imagination must have necessarily followed from this: that there is not a single image from Nature in the whole body of his works.'

The conventional language of poetry during the period from Milton to Thomson, the ' poetic diction ' against which the Preface to *Lyrical Ballads* is so spirited a protest, has its source in that habit of the poets who invented it by which they take either no images from Nature, or only such as they borrow from one another. It is with this habit that Wordsworth, early in the

Preface, contrasts his own practice in the *Lyrical Ballads*. ' I do not know', he says, ' how to give the reader a more exact notion of the style in which it was my wish and intention to write than by informing him that I have at all times endeavoured to look steadily at my subject; consequently there is, I hope, in these poems little falsehood of description.'

Throughout life Wordsworth held with passionate insistency to the belief which he here forces upon the attention of the reader of the Preface—that a true style can be founded upon no other base than a true observation of Nature (or of human character and manners). The belief was a healthy one; and nothing could have been more in season than that he should spend himself in inculcating it on the generation which he addressed. The high value which he thus assigns, in the work of poetry, to observation is, of course, only another aspect of what I have called his sensationalism, his gospel of eyes and ears. Such an insistency can, of course, prove self-defeating. The mere expression ' observation ' (of which Wordsworth is fond) may easily carry the suggestion of mechanical record; incautiously employed, it may obscure the distinction that there is between the sensibility of poets and that of common men. And often enough in reading Wordsworth the attention tends to rivet itself, as we contemplate the three-tiered pyramidal structure of the imaginative life, not upon the apex, but upon the base; not upon the work which ' passions ' at the top, but upon that, somewhat exclusively, which accomplishes itself on the lower level of sense-perception. Truly, the lower level is a wide and impressive stretch of feeling; nor is there anything in the imagination which was not previously in the senses—or as much, let it be added at once. For precisely this is the glory of the imagination—that it holds only just so much of the material of the senses as it can; or as it wants; as it wants for poetry, as it can make into poetry; or just so much, if you like, as is poetry. But Wordsworth, preaching to us always eyes and ears, too easily permits himself to be conceived as a degree careless of the consummating act of creative art. And of the nature of the interaction of what may be called the top and bottom moods of creation we may suspect, as I have hinted already, that he himself had but an incomplete assurance. The truth perhaps is that the imagination would not be what it is if we could say what it was; *si deprehenditur, perit*—its grandeur would be departed in being known. Of this grandeur Wordsworth was, in fact, not less sublimely sensible than greater poets. But he tends often to be the fanatic of his own gospel; the gospel of which he supposed his own age to stand in especial need; an age in which the work upon the top levels of poetry was not being done— indeed, could not be done—because there was no secure base in just feeling and true speech. Because of sham observation and sham diction (its effect) the pyramid was in subsidence.

Such an insistence, natural as it is, upon the importance of observation can, as I have said, easily obscure the difference of sensibility that there is as between poets and ordinary men. This is something which carries, it may be thought, no very unfortunate consequences; that a stab should be dealt to the complacency of poets by one of their own order. But in fact Wordsworth recognizes pretty liberally the line that demarcates genius and the common run of talent. He will not allow, it is true, that between the nature of the poet and the humanity of lesser men there is any difference *of kind*. The poet 'is a man speaking to men'. No other position, indeed, could he adopt which would be consistent with the democratizing march of his whole nature; with his faith alike in humble life and humble language; with his strong sympathy with the ballad literature, and, in a word, with whatever smacks of 'Nature'. Yet, if he will allow no difference of kind between poets and men, it must be conceded that he makes as wide as he can the difference of degree. The poet is a man 'endowed with more lively sensibility, more enthusiasm and tenderness; who has a greater knowledge of human nature, and a more comprehensive soul, than are supposed to be common among mankind ... who rejoices more than other men in the spirit of life that is in him'; a man 'habitually impelled to create' passions and volitions where he does not find them in Nature. 'To these qualities he has added a disposition to be affected more than other men by absent things as if they were present; an ability of conjuring up in himself passions, which are indeed far from being the same as those produced by real events ... yet do more nearly resemble the passions produced by real events than anything which ... other men are accustomed to feel.'

We have but to glance our eye down this protracted catalogue of glittering qualifications, in order to conceive the doubt whether, after all, that creature wherein they co-exist is, or can be, the same flesh and blood with ourselves. Is the sum of these differences *really* no more than a matter of degree? The fact is that Wordsworth is something of a philosophic shirker—here and elsewhere. What is it, when all is said, what is it to have 'a more comprehensive soul' than other men, to be 'habitually impelled to create', to 'feel absent things as though they were present', to 'conjure up passions' which are true to life without being like it? If to be, and have, all this does not constitute difference in kind from ordinary men, what do words mean? At the head of his catalogue Wordsworth puts the question, *What is a poet?* But he neither answers it, nor has any intention of answering it, *really*. If he had tried to do so, I suppose he would have been obliged to commit himself to some such statement as this: That the poet, in creating (which is where, for us, he matters), is to other men as imagination is to sense-perception; that is to say, he is not (or has not) more than they, but less; all those powers which he exercises proceed from a liberty which he has achieved; he has shed, in some god-given mood of tranquillity, the accidents of his feelings, creating for himself a space and air in which his mind moves unencumbered. He is greater than other men, and imagination is greater than sense, in a fashion which, paradoxically enough, is, not qualitative, but quantitative; he is greater than other men because he contains less of what he does not need, of what poetry does not need.

Something like this, I think, Wordsworth would say, or could be driven to saying, of the poet as he is when he creates, when he stands at the apex of the pyramid. But Wordsworth is always, as I have said, insistent that we should regard, not merely the apex, but the lower ranges; and it is clear that there already, and not merely on the top levels, the poet differs from other men. In the enumeration of his attributes, attention is called first to his 'more lively sensibility', secondly to his 'comprehensive soul', and lastly to his power to 'create'. We have noticed already a character of this 'sensibility' which is, for Wordsworth, all-important. It is *affectual*, it is bound up with our moral nature. And, if I understand Wordsworth rightly, it is by this *affectual* element in sensibility that the objects of sense, and the passions which they excite, are gradually purified for the imagination.

The poet, accordingly, possesses not only a 'more lively' but a more *affectioned* sensibility than other men. It is in this *affectioned sensibility* that poetry begins. To this beginning there succeeds the mood of 'emotion recollected in tranquillity', and to this the consummating creative mood when emotion labours again and is delivered. If from our figure of the pyramid, if from Wordsworth's doctrine of the three successive moods that go to poetic creation, we demand a greater substantiality of outline than is proper generally to trope, we are likely to run against, and be beaten by, difficulties: difficulties which are as old as the philosophies which first debated 'potentiality' and 'actuality', 'becoming' and 'being'. At once our three moods melt into one another, our triple tiers fade to a single face of rock. The fact is that, in the affectioned, or affectionizing, sensibility in which the poet begins, there is already implicit the sequent tranquillity, and in both moods implicit also the faculty of re-creating, under purged forms, the emotions without which poetry cannot, in Wordsworth's own phrase, be 'carried alive into the heart'. It is well, therefore, as I think, not to insist too strictly on those parts of the Preface, or of Wordsworth's poetry, which would seem to locate upon the top levels of the poet's activity that which especially distinguishes him from ordinary men. The poet, wherever we place the sources of his greatness, is not three pieces of a man, but a totality of greatness. His supreme act is seen, no doubt, when he creates; and that, while he creates necessarily out of passion, he is especially then to be called a poet because he deals in passion which has been transmuted, this it is valuable to emphasize—in Wordsworth it is, in fact, insufficiently emphasized. None the less he begins to be a poet at a point in the scale of being and feeling infinitely lower down; and it is this, and not the culminating development, which especially interests Wordsworth:

> O mystery of Man, from what a height
> Proceeds thy greatness!

This is why he has so much to say upon 'observation'.

The words 'observe' 'observation' are favourite terms with him in the notes to his poems. But in connexion with what I have said here as to the place of observation in his system, it is to be noticed that in the Preface of 1815 he distinguishes, not only between 'observation' and sensibility, but between 'poetic and human sensibility'; and in introducing these distinctions he gives us to understand that 'the character of the Poet delineated in the original Preface' (by which he means interpolated into the second edition of that Preface!) has already sufficiently marked them. It was introduced—undoubtedly—with that intention; whether it has served that intention adequately is more doubtful. The new terms are in any case less helpful than they seem. The poet brings to the work of observation 'a more lively sensibility' than other men; and when these differing sensibilities have been distinguished as 'poetic' and 'human', are we much wiser? And when, having made this distinction, Wordsworth tries to persuade us that it is one without a *difference in kind*, does he really convince either us or himself?

Of his own method and habits of observation Wordsworth has told us a good deal. To the end, he was restless both to observe and to observe himself observing —I would suggest, in parenthesis, that at a quite early date the habit of watching his own observation became an obsession with him, and that it is a habit not friendly to a 'lively sensibility'. 'It would be difficult', says his most recent anthologist,[1] 'to find a poet who has told us more about the conditions of the composition of his poetry than Wordsworth has'. The writer is thinking mainly of the information supplied by the poems themselves; and it is, indeed, remarkable to how great a degree Wordsworth, in much of his best poetry, takes us into his confidence, and allows us to penetrate the environment of his inspiration. But, apart from this, he dictated in his last years an extensive commentary upon his Collected Works—the series of 'Notes and Illustrations' usually known as the Fenwick Notes. In some of these notes his memory of circumstances is demonstrably defective. Yet of a vast number of the poems upon which he comments, he could probably have said truthfully what he says of the earliest of his longer pieces: 'There is not an image ... which I have (? had) not observed; and now, in my seventy-third year, I recollect the time and place where most of them were noticed.'[2] The poem spoken of is *An Evening Walk*. The example is an interesting one; because,

[1] Mr. D. Nichol Smith, *Wordsworth, Prose and Poetry*, p. xvi—the best 'Preliminary' to Wordsworth that there is.

[2] Fenwick Notes, p. 4. (Here and elsewhere I cite by the pages of Grosart, vol. iii.)

The Preface to 'Lyrical Ballads'

although Wordsworth has so properly emphasized the close connexion between a pure diction and just observation of Nature, the diction of the *Evening Walk* is irredeemably bad. The fact is that Wordsworth had taught *himself* to observe, but Dr. Darwin had taught him to write the *Evening Walk*; and, as yet, authority oppressed Nature. What Wordsworth tells us, however, of having carried with him for fifty and more years the memory of the times and places where most of the images of the poems were composed is arresting; not as a personal idiosyncrasy, but as illustrating what may be called the *method* of his inspiration. In his old age he had become a kind of miser of his memories, hoarding and hugging them to himself. But from the beginning, it was his purpose (a purpose imposed upon him by his whole metaphysic of the imagination) to make his mind ' a mansion for all lovely forms ', his memory

> as a dwelling place
> For all sweet sounds and harmonies.

He was waiting always, in respect of each and all of these images,[1] for the hour when the passion of the first sense-perception of any one of them should re-create itself, under a changed form, ' in the mind itself ', should become poetry.

Of the genesis of the poem called *The Thorn* the Fenwick Notes offer the following account:[2]

' Arose out of my *observing* on the ridge of Quantock Hill, on a stormy day, a Thorn, which I had often past

---

[1] Thus, in the first book of the *Prelude*, enumerating his qualifications for the work of poetry, he says:

> Nor am I naked of external things,
> Forms, images, nor numerous other aids (154–5).

[2] Fenwick Notes, p. 41.

in calm and bright weather without noticing it. I said to myself, cannot I by some invention do as much to make this Thorn permanently an impressive object as the storm has made it to my eyes at this moment?'

Take, again, this (of the *Lament of Mary Queen of Scots*):[1]

'This arose out of a flash of moonlight that struck the ground when I was approaching the steps that lead from the garden at Rydal Mount to the front of the house.'

Notes like these—I have taken two at random—are found on almost every page of the Fenwick collection. Interesting they are, and were bound to be—no other poet of equal genius has in the same degree or kind taken us into his confidence. But even so, I feel impelled to ask—does very much come of it? Or could very much come of it? Is it possible that a poet should be able to tell us all that Wordsworth is trying to tell us (and believes himself in fact to communicate to us)? Is it possible that he should, for fifty years—or for five minutes—carry, as it were, in his pocket the flash of sense in which inspiration has its obscure beginning, and be able to produce it at call? How shall he, or any one, tell us to what element in the colliding forces of the mind and of nature the Thorn-tree owes the mystery that gathers to it unpredictably out of the storm? Will a thousand Fenwick Notes bring us any nearer to the secret of

> And she is known to every star
> And every wind that blows?[2]

or bridge for us the transition from the visual image

---

[1] Fenwick Notes, p. 24.   [2] *Thorn*, 69-70.

of the moon's light along the terrace at Rydal to the magic of

> Me, unapproached by any friend—
> Save those who to my sorrow lend
> Tears due unto their own?[1]

'It is the appropriate business of poetry...', says the *Essay Supplementary*, 'to treat of things ... not as they exist in themselves, but as they seem to exist to the senses and the passions.' The remark comes from the year 1815; but it sorts with the teaching and practice of Wordsworth's earlier, his really effective, period; and it is worth a good many Fenwick Notes. That man, it might almost be said, observes most justly who observes least; *he* 'looks steadily at his object' who attends to nothing in connexion with it save the appearance which fires the senses to passion. The accurate observation of the Thorn-tree consists, not in reproducing what the Thorn-tree ordinarily, or really, is; but in the preservation (and subsequent re-creation) of that appearance of it which it cast, in an individual flash, upon an individual spirit, upon the 'passioning' senses of its poet. This is not to say more than has been urged throughout this book—that poets see things that ordinary men do not see, and that what ordinary men see *they* see in a fashion not ordinary; and that on this account are they called *seers*.

In respect of the *Lament of Mary Queen of Scots* (not in itself a notable poem), I would here, in passing, call attention to a circumstance which I have not seen noticed elsewhere. Wordsworth offers, in his account of the poem, no explanation at all of the connexion, in

[1] *Lament of Mary Queen of Scots*, 19-21.

his own mind or in historic fact, between the flash of moonlight, as he saw it on the terrace at Rydal Mount, and the fate of Mary. The source of the connexion is, I think, a poem of Helen Maria Williams, *Queen Mary's Complaint*.[1] Miss Williams was, however oddly, an object of Wordsworth's youthful enthusiasm. At sixteen he had addressed a sonnet to her; and her poems ('sent to me by the author from Paris') were among the books in his possession at his death. *Queen Mary's Complaint* opens, like Wordsworth's *Lament*, with an apostrophe to the Moon:

> Pale Moon, thy wild benignant light,
> May glad some other captive's sight.

In both poems the Queen laments at length that she ever was a queen, and reflects fondly upon the unfortunate pleasures of her youth. She speaks, in Miss Williams, of 'woes for ever doomed to last', and, in Wordsworth, of 'wounds that may not heal'; and in both, she speaks of Elizabeth as 'sister queen'. If the two poems are read together, the reader will, I think, find it difficult not to believe that the later piece was written in unconscious memory of the earlier. This matter of the moon at Rydal does in fact afford a valuable indication of the complex character of 'observation'.

Something may be added here, which will be found, I fancy, not wholly irrelevant, about Wordsworth's method and practice of *composition*. The Fenwick Notes, and other material, tell us, about his observation, all that we want to know—that is, that nothing can really be known. But if we cannot, by the help of these, hold the flash of sense, the Journals, and in a less degree the Letters of Dorothy Wordsworth enable us

[1] *Poems by Helen Maria Williams*, ed. ii, 1791, vol. ii, pp. 31 sqq.

The Preface to 'Lyrical Ballads'

to observe, in part, its after-workings; to be present, very often, with the poet himself when his imagination labours undelivered. Of Dorothy, of this 'sister of his soul', as he calls her, Wordsworth has left no memorial more charming than the poem entitled *The Butterfly*. Under date the 14th March 1802, the Journals allow us to watch the conditions under which *The Butterfly* was composed:

'William got up at nine o'clock; but before he rose he had finished *The Beggar Boy*; and while we were at breakfast he wrote the poem *To a Butterfly*. He ate not a morsel, but sate with his shirt-neck unbuttoned, and his waistcoat open, while he did it. The thought first came upon him as we were talking about the pleasure we both always felt at the sight of a butterfly. I told him that I used to chase them a little, but that I was afraid of brushing the dust off their wings, and did not catch them. He told me how he used to kill all the white ones—because they were Frenchmen. I wrote it down, and the other poems; and I read them all over to him. William began to try and alter *The Butterfly*, and tired himself.'

A letter [1] of Dorothy Wordsworth may supplement this picture of the pains of poetry:

'He is writing the poem on his own early life.... The weather, with all its pleasant mildness, has been very wet in general. He takes out the umbrella, and, I dare say, stands stock-still under it many a rainy half-hour, in the middle of road or field!'

These passages of agreeably domestic comment should be read in conjunction with Wordsworth's own description, in the fourth book of the *Prelude*, of the odd figure which he made in the countryside—and the

[1] *Letters of the Wordsworth Family*, i, p. 158.

unenviable repute which he acquired—when he walked the roads muttering his inspirations to his highland terrier:

> And when first
> The boyish spirit flagged, and day by day
> Along my veins I kindled with the stir,
> The fermentation, and the vernal heat
> Of poesy, affecting private shades
> Like a sick Lover, then this dog was used
> To watch me, an attendant and a friend,
> Obsequious to my steps early and late,
> Though often of such dilatory walk
> Tired, and uneasy at the halts I made.
> A hundred times, when, roving high and low,
> I have been harassed with the toil of verse,
> Much pains and little progress, and at once
> Some lovely image in the Song rose up
> Full-formed, like Venus rising from the sea;
> Then have I darted forwards to let loose
> My hand upon his back with stormy joy,
> Caressing him again and yet again.
> And when at evening on the public way
> I sauntered, like a river murmuring
> And talking to itself when all things else
> Are still, the creature trotted on before—
> Such was his custom—; but whene'er he met
> A passenger approaching, he would turn
> To give me timely notice, and straightway,
> Grateful for that admonishment, I hushed
> My voice, composed my gait, and, with the air
> And mean of one whose thoughts are free, advanced
> To give and take a greeting that might save
> My name from piteous rumours, such as wait
> On men suspected to be crazed in brain.[1]

Perhaps we like both Wordsworth and his sister the better for their occasional perception that, to common

[1] *Prelude*, iv. 100–30.

The Preface to 'Lyrical Ballads' 183

men, the poet, in his highest act, the act of creation, is a creature necessarily absurd. More valuable, none the less, and also not a little affecting, are those passages in the Journals and Letters which make us acquainted with the alternations of passion and listlessness, spiritual exaltation and bodily sickness, amid which not a small part of Wordsworth's poetry found birth. 'He writes with so much feeling and agitation', says Dorothy in a letter, 'that it brings on a sense of pain.'[1] And again: 'William is very industrious. His mind is always active; indeed, too much so. He overwearies himself, and suffers from pain and weakness.'[2] Repeated entries in the Journals also, impressive chiefly, perhaps, in their sum, tell the same tale; and in all periods. 'William all the morning engaged in wearisome composition.' 'William got to some ugly place, and went to bed tired out.' 'William went to bed very ill after working.' 'William got to work, *and was no worse for it*'—and so on endlessly. Poetry is called poetry because it is not prose (some dicta of Wordsworth himself notwithstanding); and it is perhaps little likely, therefore, that it should come to birth in that fashion of effortless efficiency in which M. Jourdain talked prose all his life—and never knew it. It is now becoming a commonplace of Wordsworthian criticism (though not so long ago it was a paradox) that the best of the poetry which Wordsworth has left to us obeys the law of all good poetry (as he has himself formulated it), and has its source in passion. But perhaps those who have helped to make this a commonplace have not always observed a proper circumspection in selecting their means of persuasion. In particular, I have noticed a tendency to

[1] *Letters of the Wordsworth Family*, i, p. 126.   [2] *Ib.*, p. 120.

emphasize, among the conditions in which Wordsworth endeavoured to work creatively, the suffering or restlessness or bodily ailing which Dorothy's Letters and Journals so often mention as attending the poet's efforts to compose: a tendency to emphasize these as though in these inspiration had its source. It is interesting, and valuable, to take note of these conditions; but there is some danger, I think, of interpreting them amiss. At least it is desirable that, when attention is called to them, it should be directed also at the same time to that doctrine of the 'overbalance of pleasure' upon which Wordsworth himself lays so insistent an emphasis. That poetry, that inspiration, have as their frequent concomitants distress of mind and body—this, I think, he would not have denied: else, his own heart had condemned him. But these are not—and Wordsworth never believed them to be—the health of poetry, of inspiration: but its sickness. To this sickness all inspiration is liable; and it afflicts, perhaps, the loftier imaginations more frequently and more forcibly than those of lower temper. His sister's Letters and Journals witness the degree of affliction in this kind which Wordsworth experienced. Yet he never lost faith in the doctrine that it is the function of the imagination, the supreme act of the work of making poetry, so to temper the passions in which it works that they become, for their poet, not painful, but pleasurable.

And I come here to the last clause in Wordsworth's metaphysic of poetry. 'If Nature be thus cautious', he says, in words which I have already quoted, 'if Nature be thus cautious to preserve in a state of enjoyment a being so employed, the poet ought to profit by the lesson held forth to him, and ought especially to take care that, whatever passions he communicates to his reader, those passions, if his reader's mind be sound and vigorous, should always be accompanied by an overbalance of pleasure.' It will be seen that it is the business of the poet—who works always in passion—to communicate to his reader, not that passion in which he himself began, that passion which is in the senses, but that filtrated (or 'selected') passion which, while it is 'kindred to' the other, has been made free of accident, has, as it were, put off mortality. The original impressions of sense, whatever their character, the poet feels —because he is a poet—in a fashion more lively, more poignant, than ordinary men. But—and, again, because he is a poet—he more quickly than ordinary men reestablishes his tranquillity. Presently (to-morrow, it may be, or from sources 'ten years deep') he 'passions' again. The sorrow that has slept stirs anew; but now it is

> Sorrow that is not sorrow, but delight,
> And miserable love that is not pain
> To hear of.

It is this purified passion that the poet conveys to those to whom he speaks; and hence that power which there is in poetry to console and sustain. The poet 'thinks and feels in the spirit of human passions'. *In the spirit of them*; for, once more, let there be no mistake. It is in vain that we think and feel passionately—in vain for the purposes of poetic creation—unless this passion of thought and feeling has that in it by which it spiritualizes itself. Perhaps that is only another way of saying that the work of the imagination can be done by the imagination only. Yet perhaps even so it is worth saying; for many poets, and most men, find it hard to believe.

xii

THE COMPOSITION OF 'THE PRELUDE'

THE *Advertisement* to the first edition of the *Prelude* (1850) states that the poem 'was commenced in the beginning of the year 1799, and completed in the summer of 1805'. The first part of this statement is made more explicit by a note appended to the third line of Book VII. The writer of that note supposes the 'preamble' to the poem (i. e. lines 1–45 of Book I) to have been written on the day on which Wordsworth left the German town of Goslar. This date has recently been determined exactly by the aid of (*a*) an unpublished letter of Dorothy Wordsworth, and (*b*) a document in the Archives of the municipality of Goslar (Harper, *William Wordsworth*, i, pp. 365–8). The Wordsworths left Goslar on the 23rd February 1799.

But Wordsworth himself dates the 'preamble' from a day of *autumn* (*Prelude*, i. 65), and he speaks of having composed it when he was newly 'escaped from the vast city'. At no time could Goslar be described as a *vast city*. The last edition of the *Encyclopaedia Britannica* gives its population (in 1905) as 17,000. In 1799 it can scarcely have contained half that population (in 1728 the city was a heap of ashes). Wordsworth speaks, moreover, of

>   the vast city where I long had pined
> A discontented sojourner, now free,
> Free as a bird to settle where I will (i. 7–9).

But he was in Goslar only some four months, and he had

been free to settle where he would for the last three years. It is even worth observing, perhaps, that, whereas Dorothy Wordsworth notices, as they leave Goslar, the *firwoods* of its environs (Harper, i, p. 368), lines 80 sqq. of the first book of the *Prelude* speak only of 'the stately grove of *oaks*'. This consideration will not appear trivial to any one who has remarked the frequency with which poems of Wordsworth reproduce, in matters of this kind, the detailed observation of Dorothy's Journals.

The difficulties here noticed have led most—perhaps all—recent commentators[1] to accept (with varying degrees of hesitation) a view of the 'preamble' first propounded by Mr. Thomas Hutchinson. Mr. Hutchinson conceives the 'preamble' to describe the feelings 'which possessed Wordsworth when, in the autumn of 1795, having invested Raisley Calvert's legacy, . . . he turned his back on London and set out for Bristol . . . and took possession of Racedown House'.[2] The 'vast city' is, *in fact*, London.[3]

If the editor of the *editio princeps* had not written a careless note at vii. 3, and if Wordsworth's first two biographers (Chr. Wordsworth and Professor Knight) had possessed critical alertness, it would not have taken

[1] Mr. Moore Smith (1896); Mr. Worsfold (1904); Mr. Nowell Smith (1908); Mr. Harper (1916).

[2] Cited in Mr. Nowell Smith's edition, iii, p. 567.

[3] Compare 'the great city', *Prelude*, ii. 452, viii. 626, x. 245, xiii. 114, 365; 'the huge city', vi. 267, viii. 666; 'the mighty city', vii. 723. 'The vast city' of i. 7 is, admittedly, the same as the city mentioned in vii. 3. But the title of Book VII (*Residence in London*) sufficiently explains the reference in vii. 3. Wordsworth appropriately recalls, at the point where he is entering on a description of his life in London, the happy manner of his final escape from it.

half a century to make this discovery. Nor, perhaps, would Mr. Hutchinson have been, as he seems to be, afraid to draw the necessary corollary of his discovery. While he conceives the 'preamble' to record Wordsworth's feelings on leaving London for Racedown in 1795, he nevertheless supposes it to have been actually 'composed on the day of his (Wordsworth's) departure from Goslar'.[1] But here Wordsworth himself refutes Mr. Hutchinson. If the feelings of the 'preamble' are those of 1795, then nothing can be more certain than that it was composed in 1795. Wordsworth calls special attention, in lines 46–8, to the fact that the 'preamble' is distinguished from most of his other compositions precisely by being *exactly contemporary* with the emotions it describes:

> Thus far did I, my friend, unused to make
> A present joy the matter of a song,
> Pour forth my soul that day.

The suggestion that the 'preamble' was both felt *and composed* in the autumn of 1795 was, so far as I know, first made—and only very tentatively—by Mr. Harper.[2] Mr. Harper thinks it 'possible' that lines 1–45 were composed 'at Windsor, or some other point on the Thames' where Wordsworth 'paused on his way' from London to Racedown. But the journey described by Wordsworth is

A pleasant loitering journey, through *three days*;

and it would tax the powers of Mr. Harper, or any one else, to accomplish in three days' walking the journey from Windsor (or any point on the Thames from which the 'curling cloud of city smoke' can be seen—as it cannot from Windsor) to Racedown. But here I can

---
[1] Nowell Smith, *loc. cit.*   [2] ii, pp. 144–5.

come to Mr. Harper's assistance. In the summer and autumn of 1795 Wordsworth was *probably* in London for a period—very likely, as Mr. Knight thinks,[1] a considerable period. But he was quite certainly in Bristol on the 2nd September.[2] Bristol to Racedown is a practicable three-days' saunter; and I would suggest that, while the reference in 'the vast city where I long had pined' is to London, 'the curling cloud of city smoke' upon which Wordsworth cast 'a backward glance' (i. 88-9) was the smoke of Bristol; and that the river of line 30 is neither, as Mr. Harper thinks, the Thames, nor, as most editors, the Goss, but the varied and beautiful Avon.

The country round Racedown may very well have become known to Wordsworth when he toured the west of England in the summer of 1793—we know very little of the details of his movements in that period. This would explain the expression 'a known vale' (in i. 72), which perplexes Mr. Harper. Nor need the description of Racedown as a 'cottage' (i. 74), although inaccurate, trouble us. Wordsworth speaks of 'Racedown Cottage' in a letter of the 20th November, 1795—when he was already living there. It is clear, however, from the language of i. 74 sqq. that he had not seen the 'cottage'. He speaks of

> the one cottage which methought I saw.
> *No picture of the memory ever looked*
> *So fair*; and while upon the *fancied* scene
> I gazed with growing love, a higher power
> Than *Fancy* gave assurance of some work
> Of glory forthwith there to be begun.

[1] ix, p. 103.
[2] See the letter of Dorothy Wordsworth cited by Mr. Harper, i, p. 274. The whole letter has not been published. It is referred to by Mr. Knight, *loc. cit.*

The cottage is not remembered : it has never been seen, save with the eye of Fancy.

I take the opening of the *Prelude*, then, to be a truthful and exact narrative of fact. On a fine autumn day, in September–October, 1795, about two p.m. (i. 67), Wordsworth was in the neighbourhood of Bristol, where yielding to the elation of spirits caused by his recent release from London, he poured out the ' measured strains ' (i. 1–45) which constitute the ' preamble ' to the poem. These verses, but these only, belong to the autumn of 1795. In the lines which follow them (composed at a date which we are not yet in a position to determine), he describes how, having composed the ' preamble ', he sat down in a ' green shady place ' to meditate upon the use to which he should put his new-won liberty. Suddenly the whim seized him to walk,

Even with the chance equipment of the hour,

to Racedown. His Bristol friends the Pinneys had made him the offer of their farm there, and he now took the resolution to go there. Three days brought him to his ' hermitage ' (i. 107).

This visit, undertaken on the impulse of the moment, may be conceived as a visit of inspection. The details of the more permanent settlement in the ' hermitage ' are omitted. But lines 108–269 describe the conditions of the poet's subsequent life there, its hopes, its discouragements, its interchange of zeal and listlessness.

It will be noticed that, if this analysis is a true one, nothing is said (here, or, indeed, elsewhere in the *Prelude*) of the poet's settlement in Grasmere. That settlement is narrated in the extant fragment of *The Recluse*. The majority of commentators have, it is true, supposed that this opening portion of the *Prelude* does, in fact, describe the retirement to Grasmere in 1799. But they have not explained how, if that be so, the moods which *The Recluse* depicts as developing upon the retirement to Grasmere are so completely opposed to those delineated in lines 108–269 of the first book of the *Prelude*. And in fact, the migration related in the opening portion of the *Prelude cannot* be the migration to Grasmere. Wordsworth went to live in Grasmere, not in the autumn, nor amid sunshine, but just before Christmas in bitterly inclement weather. He set out for Grasmere, not from an industrial city wreathed in clouds of smoke, but from the hamlet of Sockburn. He set out, not upon the impulse of the moment, but after due preparation; nor is it likely that Dove Cottage was, as the cottage of the opening of the *Prelude* was, merely pictured on his fancy—he must already have seen it. I say nothing of the difficulties of those commentators who have to explain how the poet is to be conceived as arriving at Dove Cottage within three days of leaving either London or Goslar.

It is, of course, not to be doubted (as we shall see presently) that the greater part of the *Prelude* was written at Grasmere. But the fact furnishes no ground for such a distortion of a quite plain narrative as would carry the poet there in the first pages of the poem.

It will escape the notice of no one that the interpretation which I have given of the opening of the first book of the poem carries with it, if it be true, important consequences. I speak of an 'interpretation', and I say 'if it be true'. But I have in fact done no more than to suppose that Wordsworth means what he says. If he does, it will follow that lines 108–269 of Book I are a very valuable, and interesting, supplement to our knowledge of his literary history. They describe the direction of his poetical ambition during the period which saw the completion of *The Borderers* and the beginnings of *Lyrical Ballads*. We are now enabled to know that during a portion of this period Wordsworth played with the idea of composing both heroic and romantic epic[1] (166–220). At other times he was drawn to more familiar matter—such as he turned to good account in *Lyrical Ballads* (221–7). But the ruling ambition of this period was towards

> some philosophic song
> Of truth that cherishes our daily life;
> With meditations passionate from the deep
> Recesses in man's heart, immortal verse
> Thoughtfully fitted to the Orphean lyre (229 sqq.).

The lines which follow describe, in a manner impressive and affecting, the contradictions of nature which the poet discovers in himself when he essays to analyse his fitness for so grandiose an undertaking: 'vague longing' and 'paramount impulse', 'timorous capacity' and prudence, proper circumspection and dilatoriness, humility and selfishness, just ambition and listlessness. Assailed by these contradictions, he feels himself to be

> Unprofitably travelling toward the grave.

It is at this point that, beginning from the earliest memories of childhood, he undertakes that review of his powers, that long, subtle, and searching self-examina-

---

[1] Lines 168–9, where he speaks of the desire to

> settle on some British theme, some old
> Romantic tale by Milton left unsung,

are especially interesting, in view of the fact that in 1815 he made an attempt in this species, viz. *Artegal and Elidure*.

The Composition of 'The Prelude'

tion, which makes the matter of the fourteen books of the *Prelude*.

The questions which the *Prelude* attempts to answer are, it will be observed, those set by the period of his residence in the West of England; and it is at least suggested by the movement of the narrative that the composition of the *Prelude* itself dates from that period. Why else should Wordsworth put this period in the forefront of his poem?—the retirement to the west country could have been related more appropriately in that part of Book XIV in which mention is made of the bequest of Raisley Calvert. As it is the poem opens with a paean in praise of the liberty which came to Wordsworth with that bequest, and its 'last word of personal concern' is the passage recording the bequest (xiv. 348 sqq.). That passage is followed by lines which seem to furnish an important clue to the date at which the *Prelude* (excluding its preamble) was begun. Having mentioned Calvert, Wordsworth bids Coleridge to

> recall to mind
> The mood in which this labour was begun.

Let Coleridge look back, he says, to the summer of 1798—

> When thou dost to that summer turn thy thoughts,
> And hast before thee all which then we were,
> To thee, in memory of that happiness,
> It will be known, by thee at least, my Friend,
> Felt, that the history of a poet's mind
> Is labour not unworthy of regard.
> To thee the work shall justify itself.
>   The last, and later, portions of this gift
> Have been prepared, not with the buoyant spirits
> That were our daily portion when we first
> Together wantoned in wild Poesy. (xiv. 408–17.)

The passage, if read carefully, would seem, I think, to place the beginnings of the *Prelude* in 1798; and it can, I think, be made probable that in the summer of that year Wordsworth had completed at least a rough draft of Book I.

We have seen that, already in the period of his residence in the West of England, Wordsworth had conceived the project of a philosophical poem. He had projected the *Recluse*. In later years he spoke of the *Prelude* as a biographical poem 'preparatory' to the *Recluse*; and the Advertisement to the *Prelude* states that it 'was intended to be introductory to the *Recluse* ... the *Recluse*, if completed, would have consisted of three parts. Of these the second part alone, viz. the *Excursion* was finished and given to the world by the Author'. (The first book of the first part of the *Recluse* was left in manuscript, and first published in 1887: 'the third part was only planned'.) But was the plan of the *Recluse* (and of the relation between that poem and the *Prelude*) as sketched by Wordsworth in 1814 that which he outlined to himself fifteen or sixteen years earlier? It can, I fancy, be shown that the *Prelude* and the *Recluse* were, in their original outline, not distinct—they were not two poems, but one, and from the failure to perceive this a good deal of confusion has arisen.

Of the extant fragment of the *Recluse* (Book I) the composition can be dated fairly exactly. It was begun after the settlement in Grasmere (which it describes). Wordsworth moved to Grasmere just before Christmas, 1799, and he seems to have begun on the *Recluse* before the beginning of the spring of 1800. This appears from lines 188 sqq.:

> But the gates of spring
> Are opened; churlish winter hath given leave
> That she should entertain for this one day,
> Perhaps for many genial days to come,
> His guests.

The passage (which should be read in its entirety) suggests a date not later than the first days of March. The whole fragment was complete, at least in draft, by April of the same year. For the conclusion[1] of it mentions that John Wordsworth is already at Dove Cottage, and that Coleridge, who arrived in April, is expected (652-61).

With respect, then, to that part of his great work which bore, and still bears, the exclusive title of the *Recluse*, there are no difficulties. It belongs to the months March-April 1800.

But there was an earlier, and more mysterious, *Recluse*. On the 6th March 1798, Wordsworth writes to John Tobin that he has written 1,300 lines of a poem designed to give ' pictures of Nature, Man and Society '. We are at once reminded of the words in which, in the Preface to the *Excursion*, Wordsworth describes the grand *Recluse* (the *Recluse* in three parts) : ' a philosophical poem, containing views of Man, Nature and Society.' And we are reminded of the first words of the piece which Wordsworth calls ' a kind of prospectus of the design and scope of the whole poem ' :

> On Man, on Nature, and on Human Life
> Musing in solitude.

By the side of this should be placed a letter written on the 11th March 1798, to James Losh. ' I have

---

[1] I say ' the conclusion of it ', because, as we shall see presently, the last 107 lines were composed at an earlier date.

been', Wordsworth there says, 'fairly industrious within the last few weeks. I have written 706 lines of a poem which I hope to make of considerable utility. Its title will be, The Recluse, or Views of Nature, Man and Society.' It is clear that by the second week of March 1798, Wordsworth had written, or drafted, some 1,300 to 2,000 lines of *a* ' Recluse ', and it seems a reasonable inference that, among these 1,300–2,000 lines, were the lines which conclude the extant *Recluse* ; the lines beginning

> On Man, on Nature, and on Human Life,

—the passage which Wordsworth calls the ' prospectus ' of the grand three-part *Recluse*.

But the ' prospectus ' does not go beyond 107 lines. What were the other 1,200–1,900 lines drafted in March 1798?

They can have been, I think, nothing but the beginnings of the *Prelude*. The time of year corresponds with the season in which we know the first book of the *Prelude* to have been begun. ' I began ', Wordsworth says,

> ere the breath of spring
> Planting my snowdrops among winter snows.
> (*Prelude*, i. 613–16).

The verses were read to, or read by, Coleridge, who writes to Cottle on the 8th March 1798:

' He (Wordsworth) has written more than 1,200 lines of a blank verse superior, I hesitate not to aver, to anything in our language which any way resembles it. Poole . . . thinks of it as likely to benefit mankind much more than anything Wordsworth has yet written.'

The verses cannot be the first book of the *Excursion*

(the 'Ruined Cottage')—that was written as early as 1797.[1] They cannot be a first draft of the extant *Recluse*, since that fragment deals with the settlement in Grasmere, nearly two years later. Nor do we know of any other poem, or part of a poem, written by Wordsworth that they can be—unless they belong to the *Prelude*. The *Prelude* never bore any title until it was christened by Mrs. Wordsworth in 1850. It was commonly spoken of by Wordsworth as 'the poem upon the growth of my mind'; and by Dorothy Wordsworth as 'the poem to Coleridge'. But more than one letter of Coleridge affords evidence that, at any rate in its inception, it was occasionally identified with, and spoken of as, the *Recluse*. 'I long to see what you have been doing,' Coleridge writes to Wordsworth on the 12th October 1799. 'O let it be the tail-piece of the *Recluse*; for of nothing but the *Recluse* can I hear patiently. That *it is to be addressed to me* makes me more desirous that it should not be a poem of itself.'[2] The *Prelude* only, and not the *Recluse*, was addressed to Coleridge; but to Coleridge, in 1798, the *Prelude was* the *Recluse*. No other *Recluse* existed.

This may be seen farther from an earlier letter of Coleridge of the same year. 'I do intreat you', he writes to Wordsworth, 'to go on with the *Recluse*; and I wish you would write a poem, in blank verse, addressed to those who, in consequence of the complete failure of the French Revolution, have thrown up all hopes of the amelioration of mankind, and are sinking into an almost

---

[1] Knight, ix, p. 112; and as late as 1804 the *Excursion* was less than 1,000 lines in length; see below, p. 206 *n*.

[2] *Ib.*, p. 201. By 'a poem of itself' Coleridge means one of the 'small poems' which he elsewhere warns Wordsworth against.

epicurean selfishness, disguising the same under the soft titles of domestic attachment and contempt for visionary *philosophes*. It would do good, and might form a part of the *Recluse*.'

It did form a part of the *Recluse*—that is to say, of the *Prelude*. M. Legouis has long since pointed out how in the penultimate paragraph of the second book of the *Prelude* Wordsworth has taken these sentences of Coleridge and versified them (see especially, lines 434–40).

I suggest, then, that the composition of the *Prelude* dates from the early part of the year 1798.[2] Before the end of March, Wordsworth had drafted some 1,200–1,900 lines of it. That these were 1,200–1,900 lines of continuous composition, we need not necessarily believe —a great deal of Wordsworth's writing was done in disconnected patches, which were afterwards united to a larger whole. It seems, however, clear from lines 612 sqq. of the first book that that book was substantially[3] complete before the end of the year in which it was begun—perhaps by the autumn of 1798. Book II affords no indication of date beyond that furnished by the second of the two letters of Coleridge just quoted. The conclusion of the book cannot have been written earlier than the summer of 1799, nor—when we remember how impermanent is the stimulus of a friend's letter—much later. It may be taken as roughly contemporaneous with the letter which it, in part, versifies.

[1] Knight, ix, p. 195.

[2] The 'preamble' being, however, a waif from the autumn of 1795.

[3] i. 401–62 were, if Wordsworth's later memory is to be trusted, written in Germany. No doubt much that had been written in the early part of 1798 received revision in Germany.

The Composition of 'The Prelude' 199

Consonant with this are the words of farewell addressed to Coleridge in lines 466 sqq. It was in July 1799 that Wordsworth abandoned the idea of settling near Coleridge in the neighbourhood of Stowey.[1]

Book III contains no clear indications of date. But that some portion of it was written under the same stimulus as that which completed Book II, and is roughly contemporaneous with the end of Book II, is at least suggested by the language in which Coleridge is addressed at iii. 197 sqq.:

> So be it, if the pure in heart be prompt
> To follow, and if thou, my honoured friend,
> *Who in these thoughts art ever by my side*,
> Support, as heretofore, my fainting steps.

The words italicized would most naturally come from a point of time not very distant from the farewell to Coleridge which concludes the second book: perhaps the winter of 1799. The suggestion is borne out by other, and more concrete, evidence. At the end of 1799 Wordsworth moved to Grasmere, and the interest of the *Prelude* was thereon replaced by the composition of the extant *Recluse*,[2] and of the twenty-two new poems [3] which during 1800 were added to *Lyrical Ballads* (an enlarged edition of which appeared in January 1801). The year 1801 was, of the whole period of Wordsworth's greatness, the most barren, almost the most barren of his life. Perhaps Mary Hutchinson, whom he married in the following year, had something to do with this: she was at Dove Cottage for some three months. A part

[1] Dykes Campbell, *Life of Coleridge*, p. 101, n. 4.

[2] 'I grieve that the *Recluse* sleeps,' Coleridge writes in February 1800 (C. Wordsworth, *Memoirs*, i, p. 160). He means the *Prelude*—the *Recluse* proper was just waking into life.

[3] Among them a poem of some compass and elaboration, *Michael*.

of the year also (as we have only recently learned [1]) was given to a tour in Scotland. In any case nothing was done at the *Prelude*, beyond what may be inferred from two isolated entries in Dorothy Wordsworth's Journal, the first on December 26: 'William wrote part of the poem to C(oleridge)'; and the second on the 27th December: 'Mary wrote some lines of the third part of his poem' (apparently the *Prelude*). There is a similar isolated reference in the Journal on the 11th January 1803: 'William was working at his poem to C(oleridge).' But apart from these references, there is no mention, in the Journal or elsewhere, of any work upon the *Prelude* until the beginning of 1804; and in the opening lines of Book VII Wordsworth himself says plainly that, after the first rush of inspiration which gave birth to the poem, there was

> a less impetuous stream
> That flowed awhile with unabated strength,
> Then stopped for years; not audible again
> Before last primrose-time:

—before, that is, the early months of 1804. The 'less impetuous stream' I take to be the greater part of Books I–III, and the years during which this stream was 'stopped' the whole of the years 1800–3. Early in 1804 Wordsworth writes to his friend Wrangham [2] that he is engaged on a poem on his 'earlier life', 'which will take five parts, or books, to complete; *three of which are nearly finished.*' The letter is not exactly dated, but belongs probably to the month of February.[3] For on the eighth of that month, Coleridge,

---

[1] Harper, ii, pp. 5–6.
[2] *Letters of the Wordsworth Family*, i, p. 156.
[3] It must be posterior to January 23, for it speaks of Coleridge

in a letter [1] to Wordsworth and his sister, exclaims: 'Oh, for one hour of the *Recluse*'—he has evidently heard that, since he left Grasmere, work upon the *Prelude* has recommenced. On the 13th February Dorothy [2] writes that her brother is 'writing the poem on his own early life, which is to be an appendix to the *Recluse*'; and on the 6th March the poet himself tells De Quincey that the poem is 'better than half complete, four books, amounting to about 2,500 lines'.[3] The four books here spoken of, and the three mentioned in the letter to Wrangham, need not, perhaps, be supposed to correspond *exactly* in their divisions with those which we now have,[4] and probably excisions and additions were made before 1807. But since the first four books, as we have them, contain 2,218 lines, the correspondence is fairly close—Wordsworth's figure, 2,500 is, confessedly, only approximate. On the 24th March Dorothy Wordsworth mentions [5] that 'a great addition to the poem on my brother's life has been made since C(oleridge) left us—fifteen hundred lines'. Coleridge left Grasmere

as in London, and he only arrived in London on that day. It cannot be later than the 18th February, on which day Coleridge left London (Dykes Campbell, *Life*, p. 141).

[1] *Letters of S. T. C.*, p. 459.
[2] *Letters of the Wordsworth Family*, i, p. 159.
[3] *Ib.*, p. 162. See also *ib.* iii, pp. 459-60.
[4] The present division into books was perhaps not made final until 1839, when Wordsworth revised the whole poem, during February–March. (Both Mr. Knight and Mr. Worsfold speak of a revision in 1832: perhaps by a misprint—at least I know no evidence of the work having been revised in that year.) In January 1807, when the poem was 'finished', Coleridge, to whom it had just been read entire, spoke of it as containing thirteen (and not, as now, fourteen) books (*Memorials of Coleorton*, i, p. 213); and as late as the 1st July 1832, he knew only of thirteen books (*Table Talk*, Oxford ed., 1917, p. 188).
[5] *Letters of the Wordsworth Family*, i, p. 164.

on the 10th January. On the 29th April Wordsworth writes to Richard Sharp[1] as follows:

'I have been very busy these last ten weeks; having written between 2,000 and 3,000 lines—accurately near 3,000—in that time; namely four books and a third of another, of the poem, which I believe I mentioned to you, on my own early life. I am at present in the seventh book of this work, which will turn out far longer than I ever dreamed of.' (When he wrote to Wrangham in February he had designed to complete the poem in five books; but, as he wrote to Sir G. Beaumont,[2] in connexion with the later progress of the *Prelude*, he was not a man of sufficient 'address' to confine his motions to a narrow compass.)

The information here furnished may be to some extent supplemented from the *Prelude* itself. From lines 48–9 of Book VI,

> Four years and thirty told this very week
> Have I been now a sojourner on earth,

it would appear that by the first week in April five books[3] had been completed. The composition of the fifth book, therefore (it follows from the letter to De Quincey), falls within the limits of the 7th March to the 7th April. From a comparison of the letter to Wrangham with the letter to De Quincey it would appear, further, that Book III was finished, and the whole of Book IV written, between the beginning of February and the 6th of March. Now we have seen that the four books

---

[1] Knight, x, p. 19.   [2] *Memorials of Coleorton*, i, p. 84.
[3] Coleridge sailed for Malta on the 9th April, and he carried with him five books of the *Prelude*, which Dorothy had copied for him— and lost them! See *Letters of the Wordsworth Family*, i, p. 196; and cf. p. 164.

written up to the 6th of March correspond roughly in their dimensions with the first four books as we have them (Wordsworth's figure is, in fact, 282 lines in excess of the number now extant). Books V and VI together contain 1,483. But on the 29th April, when he speaks of himself as 'in the seventh Book', he claims to have written nearer 2,000 than 2,500 lines in the 'last ten weeks' (which would bring us back, on a strict reckoning—no doubt the expression is loosely used—to the 17th February). If to the 1,483 lines of Books V and VI we add the 469 lines of Book IV and the last 260 of Book III, and to these add the difference (282 lines) between the extant Books I–IV and the sum of those four books as given by Wordsworth in March 1804, we get a total of some 2,500 lines. But the work on the poem was resumed somewhat earlier than the 17th February, and we must therefore suppose that on the 29th April a *considerable portion* of Book VII was already drafted. The introduction to Book VII attests, of itself, that it was composed in the autumn of 1804. It also attests that from the spring to the autumn of that year the poem was altogether laid aside, and this is corroborated by Wordsworth's letters.[1] We must suppose, then, that when, in the autumn, he resumed his task, he had in hand a substantial portion of Book VII, and that this was now redrafted and the introductory portion added.

We have had some concern already with the first lines of this book, and this will perhaps be the most suitable place to deal with a difficulty in connexion with them of which (in order not to confuse farther a

[1] See e. g. *Memorials of Coleorton*, i, p. 74.

confused subject) I have deliberately refrained from speaking.

> Six changeful years have vanished since I first
> Poured out (saluted by that quickening breeze
> Which met me issuing from the City's walls)
> A glad preamble to this Verse.   (vii. 1–4.)

The lines belong to a context which, beyond question, dates from 1804.[1] The city mentioned in line 3 is, we have seen reason to believe, London, and the mention of it is motived by the fact that, in this book, Wordsworth proposes to deal with his life in London (in 1792–3 and 1795). But it is difficult not to believe that the reference to the 'preamble' is intended to fulfil another purpose. I cannot but feel that Wordsworth meant by it to date the beginning of the composition of the *Prelude*—just as, in what follows, he dates its progress. He wishes to say (what, if the considerations I have adduced, possess any validity, is quite true) that six years have passed since he began the *Prelude*. But he has lapsed into an easily intelligible carelessness. Instead of saying that six years have gone by since he began the *Prelude*, he has been betrayed into saying that it is six years since he poured out the 'preamble'. The 'preamble' is, it is true, the beginning of the *Prelude*, but it is so only as a quotation standing in the forefront of the poem. Its *actual* date is, as we have seen, the year 1795. The confusion into which the poet has lapsed was, perhaps, facilitated by the fact that the introduction to Book VII was (as appears from Wordsworth's letter of the 29th April 1804) an afterthought: a product of revision and reshaping. It is worth remembering that, as has been already remarked, he had

[1] This is made certain by lines 11–18.

a habit of composing in patches—patches which at a later date he would incorporate (not always skilfully) in some larger whole for which they were not originally designed. Something of the kind may conceivably have happened here.

From the end of the spring to the beginning (at least) of the autumn of 1804 the *Prelude* lay idle:

> Through the whole summer have I been at rest,
> Partly from voluntary holiday,
> And part through outward hindrance,

the poet says (vii. 16 sqq.). The reference in the last line I take to be to the domestic unsettlement occasioned by the birth of a daughter (16th August): at least I know of no other disturbing factor in the summer of 1804. On the 8th September Wordsworth writes to Sir G. Beaumont thus:

> 'I have been busily employed lately. I wrote one book of the *Recluse*, nearly a thousand lines, then had a rest. Last week I began again, and have written three hundred more. I hope all tolerably well, and certainly with good views.'

Mr. Harper [1] supposes that by 'the *Recluse*' we are here to understand the *Prelude*. But Wordsworth himself nowhere after 1798 speaks of the *Prelude* by this name. Moreover, the 1,300 lines which were finished by the 8th September can hardly have been begun later than the end of July or the beginning of August (Wordsworth's rate of composition is never ahead of that), and the letter would thus contradict the statement in Book VII that nothing was done at the *Prelude* throughout the summer. Nor again does any book of the *Prelude* run to 1,000 lines—the average length of a book

[1] ii, p. 78

works out at 560 lines odd (the longest book is vi—778 lines, the shortest xii—335 lines). On the other hand all the books of the *Excursion*, with the exception of the two last, are either over a thousand, or just short of a thousand, lines in length. I have no doubt, therefore, that the poem referred to in this letter is the *Excursion*,[1] and that Wordsworth speaks of it by its official sub-title (which, in fact, appears on the title-page of the first edition). Similarly, it must be of the *Excursion* that he speaks when, in another letter to Sir G. Beaumont[2] (1st August 1805) he says that he has 'returned to the *Recluse*' and 'written 700 additional lines' (the *Prelude* was finished by the 19th May 1805). In neither letter, of course, can the reference be to the extant *Recluse*—there is no ground for supposing that the fragment was at any time carried beyond its present dimensions.

We have, in fact, no further information about the progress of the *Prelude* until Christmas Day, 1804. On that day Wordsworth writes to Sir G. Beaumont[3] that, in the last ten weeks (i. e. since the middle of October), he has added 'upwards of two thousand lines' to the *Prelude*, and that he expects 'to have finished before the month of May' (when Coleridge, to whom the poem is addressed, was expected home). Work must, in fact, have been resumed somewhat before the middle of October; since it is almost certain that, by the date

[1] Book II and a part of III. The point is not unimportant, since the composition of Book II is usually placed in 1802. But Wordsworth, five months after he had written these 1,300 lines, writes that the whole has not got beyond 'about 2,000 lines' (*Letters*, i, p. 173). From the letter to Beaumont of the 1st August 1805 it follows that Book III was finished at that date (it is commonly supposed to have been begun four years later).

[2] *Letters of the Wordsworth Family*, i, p. 196.

[3] *Ib.*, p. 173.

at which this letter was written, Wordsworth had completed Book XI. The end of Book XI speaks of Coleridge as being in Sicily, and Coleridge left Syracuse in November 1804. Two months later, on a day in February not specified, 'My poem advances', Wordsworth writes to Sharp,[1] 'quick or slow, as the fit comes; but I wish sadly to have it finished, in order that, after a reasonable respite, I may fall to my principal work' (*sc*. the *Recluse*). This letter must belong to the first week in February, for it makes no mention of the tragic death—which occurred on the 5th February, of the poet's brother, John Wordsworth. When the news of this event came, Wordsworth 'had a strong impulse to write a poem which should record' his brother's virtues. 'I composed much, but it is all lost except a few lines. . . . Unable to proceed with this work, I turned my thoughts to the poem on my own life, and you will be glad to hear that I have added 300 lines to it in the course of last week. Two more books will conclude it. It will be not much less than 9,000 lines.' So he writes[2] to Sir G. Beaumont on the 1st May 1805. The 300 new lines were, I think, pretty certainly, the 335 lines of Book XII.[3] This would have brought the poem to over 7,000 lines; and only so, and even then with exaggeration, could Wordsworth have apprehended that two additional books would bring the whole within near distance of 9,000 lines—but, no doubt, he exaggerates intentionally (9,000 lines, he says, and adds 'not hundred, but thousand, lines'). In this connexion the conclusion of Book XII is not a little affecting. Under

[1] *Ib.*, p. 182. [2] *Ib.*, p. 185.
[3] Shortly after February he had sent to Sir G. Beaumont lines 1–69 of Book VIII, but these afford no indication of date, being extracted as 'standing more independent of the rest of the poem than perhaps any other part' (*ib.*, p. 213).

THE PRELUDE,

OR

GROWTH OF A POET'S MIND;

AN AUTOBIOGRAPHICAL POEM;

BY

WILLIAM WORDSWORTH.

LONDON:
EDWARD MOXON, DOVER STREET.

1850.

[*reduced*]

The Composition of 'The Prelude'

stress of his recent calamity, the poet's mind travels back, and he carries the reader to the recollection of a day in the year 1783, when he journeyed home—' my brothers and myself', he says, pathetically—for the Christmas holidays:

> ere we had been ten days
> Sojourners in my father's house, he died,
> And I and my three brothers, orphans then,
> Followed his body to the grave. (xii. 306 sqq.)

The lines need no comment, but it is a pity that commentators should read them and miss the circumstance which gave birth to them.

In the last week of April, when he wrote these lines, Wordsworth had intended, as he tells Sir G. Beaumont, to add two more books to his poem, and he must have meant them, together, to mount to some 1,500 or more verses. He seems, in fact, to have added one book only, for, as we have noticed already, there were only *thirteen* books in 1807. The one book added no doubt consisted of the present Books XIII and XIV, not then separated, and together making 832 lines. The whole task was completed towards the end of May: on the 3rd June, Wordsworth writes [1] to Sir G. Beaumont:

'I have the pleasure to say that I finished my poem about a fortnight ago. I had looked forward to the day as a most happy one; and I was indeed grateful to God for giving me life to complete the work, such as it is. But it was not a happy day for me: I was dejected on many accounts. . . . I ought to add that I have the satisfaction of finding the present poem not quite of so alarming a length as I apprehended.'

The mood of dejection which Wordsworth here speaks of as affecting him on the completion of his task had its source, he tells Sir G. Beaumont, partly in the recent

[1] *Letters of the Wordsworth Family*, i, p. 190.

calamity of his brother's death—the poem itself advertises us, in its last paragraphs, that it was written

> under pressure of a private grief
> Keen and enduring; (xiv. 419-20.)

but partly also in the poet's own sense that the poem was 'so far below what I seemed capable of executing'. In 1739, and perhaps at other periods, he subjected it to a considerable degree of revision. I have seemed to myself to detect at more than one place in Book III (Cambridge) the nervous motions of a revising hand. Scarcely a month after that book was first drafted, Wordsworth wrote to De Quincey, then an undergraduate at Oxford, a letter[1] earnest and eloquent upon the possible perils of his situation. No one, I fancy, who reads that letter concomitantly with Book III of the *Prelude* will escape the suspicion that the book, as we now have it, has been a good deal revised. 'Cambridge is greatly improved', Wordsworth tells De Quincey, 'since the time I was there. . . . The manners of the young men were very frantic and dissolute at that time. . . . I need not say to you that there is no true dignity but in virtue and temperance, and, let me add, chastity.' Those few lines to De Quincey tell us more about the Cambridge of Wordsworth's time than the reader will divine from the extant third book of the *Prelude*.

But if we suspect revision here, we may know it with certainty elsewhere. In Book XIII, speaking of the wandering over Salisbury Plain which gave birth to the poem *Guilt and Sorrow*, Wordsworth says to Coleridge:

> Thou, O friend,
> Pleased with some unpremeditated strains
> That served those wanderings to beguile, hast said

[1] *Letters of the Wordsworth Family*, i, p. 162.

That then and there my mind had exercised
Upon the vulgar forms of present things,
The actual world of our familiar days,
Yet higher power; had caught from them a tone,
An image, and a character, by books
Not hitherto reflected.   (xiii. 352 sqq.)

In this passage Wordsworth not only makes clear allusion to, he in effect quotes and versifies, a portion of the fourth chapter of Coleridge's *Biographia Literaria*.[1]

Despite these evidences of revision, I am not able to persuade myself (as will have been inferred from the general tenor of the essay immediately preceding) that the *Prelude* was revised by Wordsworth after 1807 in such a fashion as to do detriment, in essential matters, to its original purity of outline. In particular, I cannot bring myself to believe—with Mr. Harper, if I understand Mr. Harper aright—that the doctrine of the relation between the senses and the imagination (which is the philosophic heart of the poem) is, to an appreciable degree, sicklied with the taint of posthumous theorizing. It is part of the whole web and woof of the poem, and it is, I believe, beyond the power of the most ingenious criticism to disentangle later and earlier elements.

I may add that the mere figures which I have furnished as to the number of lines in the drafts of 1804-5 are in themselves some guarantee that what later changes Wordsworth made were of a kind not seriously to disturb the text.

---

[1] pp. 58-9 in vol. i of Mr. Shawcross' edition. I had made this observation myself before finding, with pleasure, that it had already been made by Mr. Nowell Smith.

xiii

DOROTHY WORDSWORTH

I CANNOT bring myself to take leave of Wordsworth without something said of his sister; a woman of noble character and fine sensibility, who has this claim at least upon the affections of students of poetry, that she was the guardian angel of two of the greatest of English poets. In that accommodating Valhalla of British distinction, the *Dictionary of National Biography*, a place has been found for several Wordsworths who do not matter; but none for Dorothy. This gap may one day, perhaps, be filled. What follows is neither biography nor criticism; neither portrait nor sketch nor caricature; but in truth a tribute of affection, which, as such, may be forgiven if it wants method and coherence. And indeed, I seem to have observed in students of Wordsworth, what I have not always found in students of other literature, a charity which they bear to almost everybody whom nature or accident has connected with the subject of their study. Anybody is interesting to them who at any time was near to Wordsworth; and about these fortunate persons anything that is said, even if it might have been said better, is at least taken in good part.

Dorothy Wordsworth was born upon Christmas Day of the year 1771—the year which saw the death of Gray, and the birth of Scott; and she died on the 25th January, 1855, in the year which witnessed the publication of Tennyson's *Maud* and Matthew Arnold's *Poems* : *Second*

Series. The dullness of dates is sometimes intriguing: as a girl she might have talked with Dr. Johnson, and in her last years with Mr. Bridges. Those last years, in fact, lie outside record, and almost beyond reach of pity. This 'Child of Nature', for whom in her vigorous and vivid youth her brother had prophesied, in one of the most beautiful of his shorter poems,

> an old age serene and bright
> And lovely as a Lapland night,

was destined to live the last five-and-twenty years of her life with reason clouded irrecoverably and limbs that refused their function. The picture of Rydal Mount in 1850 calls up strange and affecting thoughts. Wordsworth was eighty, Mrs. Wordsworth within a few months of eighty, Dorothy but a year younger. Wordsworth's work had been, in effect, finished more than forty years since; he had outlived, first ridicule, and then, not indeed his fame, but his vogue. Of the two women who, together, had lived with him, and for him, in Grasmere for nearly half a century, with scarce an absence, only one was still able to serve him; and their daughter Dora, the darling of the poet's age, had already passed three years before 'from sunshine to the sunless land '—like the passing of the sunshine itself. Mrs. Wordsworth outlived her husband by nine years. In comparison with Dorothy, she has perhaps not had from lovers of Wordsworth her sufficient praise; but upon her unaided, undepressed spirit fell the burden of those last years at Rydal. Like Milton, Wordsworth sometimes, it is to be feared, used the women about him as drudges; only let that never be said without its proper qualification. Its proper qualification is supplied by a passage from what I have always thought the noblest letter in all his correspondence. 'Dearest Mary,' he writes to his wife, on the 5th July, 1837, 'Dearest Mary, when I have felt how harshly I often demean myself to you, my inestimable fellow-labourer . . . I often pray to God that he would grant us both life, that I may make some amends to you for that and all my unworthiness. But you know into what an irritable state this over-strained labour often put my nerves. My impatience was ungovernable, as I *then* thought, but I now feel that it ought to have been governed. You have forgiven me, I know, as you did then; and perhaps that somewhat troubles me the more.' 'I say nothing of this to you, dear Dora,' he adds, 'though you also have had some reason to complain.'[1] That letter of Wordsworth's old age has something of the greatness of the poetry of his youth. The same perfect sincerity characterizes each and all of those occasional pieces which he addressed to his wife in verse. Two of these—'O dearer far than life and light are dear,' and 'She was a phantom of delight,' are too well known to quote, and too perfect to require comment. Two others are oddly gauche; but just to their awkward simplicity they owe what poetry they have:

> Let other bards of angels sing,
> Bright suns without a spot;
> But thou are no such perfect thing:
> Rejoice that thou art not!
>
> Heed not tho' none should call thee fair;
> So, Mary, let it be
> If nought in loveliness compare
> With what thou art to me.

Whether most women would like to be written to in such a strain, I cannot say; but I fancy that Mrs. Words-

[1] *Letters*, iii, p. 136.

worth liked this better than better poetry—or better love-making. The same may be conjectured of the companion poem to it: in which 'Such beauty as you have', he tells Mrs. Wordsworth, is, in large part, 'my fancy's own creation'. Yet, 'Be pleased,' he says, with naïve self-complacency,

> Be pleased that Nature made thee fit
>   To feed my heart's devotion,
> By laws to which all forms submit
>   In sky, air, earth and ocean.

What Mrs. Wordsworth said to this, I know very well. I know it from a conversation recorded upon another occasion. 'And I must tell you,' said Wordsworth to Miss Fenwick, 'what Mary said when I was dictating to her this morning: 'Well, William, I declare you are cleverer than ever'; and the tears started into his eyes, and he added: 'It is not often that I have had such praise: she has always been sparing of it.'[1]

Mrs. Wordsworth had not the brilliant parts of Dorothy.

> A woman good without pretence,
> Blest with plain reason and with sober sense,

she was content to think of her husband as 'clever'. Her character is given in Pope's epitaph on Mrs. Corbet, from which the two lines which I have just quoted are taken; and I cannot forbear to add Dr. Johnson's supreme comment on that character: 'a character not discriminated by any shining or eminent peculiarities; yet that which really makes, though not the splendour, the felicity of life, and that which every wise man will choose for his final and lasting companion in the languor

[1] Harper, ii. 407.

of age, in the quiet of privacy, when he departs weary
and disgusted from the ostentatious, the volatile and
the vain ... a character which the dull overlook, and
the gay despise.'

I have half-forgotten—forgiveably, I fancy—that I
set out to speak, not of Wordsworth's wife, but of his
sister. That these two women ever entertained any
small jealousy of one another, I have never heard it
whispered. ' There never lived on earth a better woman
than Mary Hutchinson,' Dorothy wrote to her friend
Jane Pollard; but she dreaded 'that concentration of
all tender feelings, past, present, and future' which
would come upon her on the day on which her brother
married; and she seems, indeed, to have been unable
to trust herself in the church. ' I slept a good deal of
the night, and rose fresh and well in the morning. A
little after eight I saw them go down the avenue to the
church. William had parted from me upstairs ... I kept
myself as quiet as I could, but when I saw the two men
running up the walk to tell us it was over, I could stand
it no longer, and threw myself on my bed, where I lay
in stillness, neither hearing nor seeing anything.' ' To
tell us it was over ' ! You might think that William had
walked down the avenue to the scaffold! Bride and
bridegroom *and Dorothy* started within an hour for
Grasmere, in one postchaise. If Dorothy felt *de trop*,
she has never said so; and if Mrs. Wordsworth felt her
to be so, she too kept her secret. As for William, at
their first halt he wrote a sonnet to the setting sun.
But these three, who had been brought up together as
children, were destined to be together under one roof
for almost half a century. The elements of the ludicrous
in this marrying and home-coming and housekeeping,

any fool can see ; and the peril of it, any sensible person easily divine. But a wise man will know that he is looking at a household of the Olympians, and will comport himself accordingly. If the household had a scold, it was Wordsworth. But the pains of poetry hurt more than common men know; and the voice of this scold comes to us with the all-condoning accent of poetry in the words I have already quoted—' I often pray to God that he would grant us both life, that I may make some amends to you for that and all my unworthiness.'

Wordsworth published, among his own poems, three little poems of Dorothy: ' the work of a female friend ' he calls them, and adds: ' if anyone regard them with dislike or be disposed to condemn them, let the censure fall upon him who, trusting in his own sense of their merit and their fitness for the place which they occupy, extorted them from the authoress.' ' Rather high and mighty ' Mr. Harper calls this; forgetting that, at least to Dorothy, Wordsworth *was* high and mighty, high and mighty as Milton or the Bible. I suspect that Dorothy read these awkward compliments to ' a female friend ' with no common delight; and what does anything else matter? It is not the business of criticism to intrude its imperfect sympathies amid a harmony of souls that no accident of maladroitness could by any possibility impair. Dorothy's three ' short pieces ' are certainly more easily condemned than disliked. One of them is a pretty enough child's lullaby; and the worst that can be said of any of them is that, happily conceived, they are executed with a conscious dependence upon Wordsworth himself, and only half succeed in a manner in which he himself more often failed than not.

We need not much deplore this—indeed, if it were

otherwise, it would be unnatural; and it may suffice
for us, as it did for Dorothy, that she should be, not
a poetess, but the sister of a poet. It is no small thing
that, at many points, she interprets Wordsworth to us
as no one else does; and a very great thing that she
was so often able to interpret him to himself. To her,
as to Mrs. Wordsworth and Dora, he was sometimes
rough in speech and manner. ' I was melancholy ' she
writes ' and could not talk, but at last I eased my heart
by weeping—" nervous blubbering " says William. It
is not so.' I like there the confident counter-assertion,
which yet implies no criticism of William. ' It is not
so '—she is content to be barely truthful; and this bare
truthfulness harbours no small resentments. The tears
of which this passage speaks were tears shed—like so
many others—for Coleridge. Recently the curtain has
been lifted a little—and indeed enough—upon the puzzle
of Dorothy's feelings towards Coleridge. There is
nothing to hide, and at the same time Dorothy has not
that commanding place in the history of our poetry
which should excuse prying. ' Thy true friend and mine '
Wordsworth says of her, speaking to Coleridge.[1] We
might well leave it at that. What more Wordsworth
either knew or guessed, we cannot say. From the ' puny
thwarting and unintermitting dyspathy ' of his wife,
from the torture of himself, from a mind and body ' that
did him grievous wrong ', Dorothy was destined to see
Coleridge seek relief in wretched attentions paid to
Mrs. Wordsworth's sister. But he is still always ' dear
Coleridge ', ' dearest Coleridge '—at the worst ' poor
Coleridge '; and it is her grand merit that she judged
genius always more truly than the world does. Mrs.

[1] *Prelude*, vi, 200.

Coleridge has found, and, no doubt, deserved, champions, and of many harsh things that have been said about Coleridge, his best friends have little title to complain. It is easy to rail at Coleridge, and to ridicule Wordsworth; and if any one does either, foolish to take offence. But Dorothy knew greatness when she saw it; and it was enough for her to be throughout life the single-hearted servant of the greatness of these two great men.

Coleridge, in his vivid fashion, spoke of the Wordsworths and himself, in the old Racedown days, as being 'three persons and one soul'; and it may be doubted whether the annals of literature hold record of such another perfect partnership. For the gaucherie of Wordsworth's 'high and mighty' references (in 1815) to the humble work of his 'female friend' does not, as I have said, really matter, if we are sensible. To neither of these two men, as, in that period of their marvellous youth, they explored 'the mighty world of eye and ear' and the mind of man, to neither of them did it ever occur to think of Dorothy as of a woman who was in the way, whose place was with cooking and mending; but wherever their feet or their fancy took them she went before them like 'a kind of gentler spring'.

This perfect partnership is prettily illustrated by Coleridge's habit of writing a letter, not to Wordsworth or his sister, but to both at once—'Dear William and Dorothy.' His poem *Dejection*, again, was addressed, as he first drafted it, to Wordsworth. Later he altered 'blameless poet' to 'virtuous Lady', throughout addressing Dorothy; and what is interesting is that the change in the person addressed necessitates no other alteration that is material. What the one has, the other has; what may be said to either, may be said to both. So much were brother and sister one soul that persons who knew them far less intimately than Coleridge occasionally imitated him in addressing them together—Lamb begins a letter ' My dear Wordsworth, or Dorothy rather '.[1] Nor, again, was there any page of Dorothy's Journals so intimate that it was not open to her brother. Indeed, ' brother and sister ', says Professor Knight, ' made use of the same note-book—some of Wordsworth's own verses having been written by him in his sister's journal '.

A partnership in things of the mind, let us not forget, was, in this period, not common between women and men; and that two youths bubbling with rebellious genius should share their every thought with the sister of one of them is something new, and has not perhaps been repeated. The pains which Dorothy in fact took to make herself fit for this partnership are worth remarking. She taught herself French, without which her brother's dearest enthusiasms were meaningless to her; with his aid she read Italian—together they spelt out Ariosto and Davila's History of the French Civil Wars. They read German together—but here it would seem that William was less enthusiastic than his sister; one of the books was Lessing; and one fancies that Dorothy hunted here communion with Coleridge rather than with her brother. What is important, however, is that her range in language and literature was at least wider than that of most casual students of poetry even to-day. That she was at home everywhere in those parts of the literature of our own country from which Wordsworth deduced, in however limited and dogmatic a fashion, the principles of good writing, whether in prose or poetry,

[1] *Letters*, No. 138 Lucas.

Dorothy Wordsworth

goes without the saying. It may, indeed, be inferred from her journals that, just as Wordsworth never *wrote*, save by Dorothy's hand (reinforced later by the other women of his family), so he *read* always by Dorothy's eyes. This has a special significance; in so far as it means that Wordsworth made poetry and judged it always by the ear; and it would be interesting, if it were possible, to trace the reactions of this circumstance upon his style—they need not all have been in the direction of improvement. But I am concerned here, not with that, but with recalling that Dorothy, to a quick and penetrating disposition of nature, added effects of study not often aimed after either by women or by girls, in an age when some of the liveliest feminine minds were singularly ill-furnished. She was four years the senior of Miss Austen; and her life was lived in an environment even more limited in its range of incident and society. Both were singularly shrewd observers. But if Miss Austen ever observed nature, she has kept it to herself; if she ever read in history or literature, she remained singularly unaffected by what might be supposed to be the benefits of doing so—perhaps indeed no writer comparable in repute was ever so empty both of knowledge and ideas.[1] Dorothy Wordsworth recalls her sex to an ideal which powerfully influenced our literature in its greatest period; like many of the women of the Elizabethan age she thought it natural that women should fit themselves for the companionship of men by a good education.

This in her is, I believe, quite as well worth emphasizing as the gift of temperament; and less easily miscon-

---

[1] Mrs. Coleridge lamented Wordsworth's 'disregard' for Jane Austen, and attributed it to his want of humour. Other explanations of it are possible.

ceived. The student of temperament often brings from his study, not what he finds, but what it is thought proper that he should have found. We have had occasion already to observe Dorothy weeping. That was in connexion with Coleridge; she is not the first, or last, person to weep in that high cause; and she had better reason than the rest. There were tears in plenty, again, on her brother's wedding-day. Nor were they wanting in less personal causes. The first time that her eyes saw the sea, they poured floods of tears. Neither she nor her brother could read together the eleventh book of *Paradise Lost* without tears. And there are other 'sentimentalities' which I need not catalogue. I mention them only to forestall misconstruction. Whatever she was, Dorothy was not a sentimentalist; indeed, if there had been latent either in her or in her brother the seeds of that kindly ailment, the poetry of Wordsworth had lacked most of those qualities which make it unlike that of the poets most like him. The truth is that, in the outward expression of emotion, there are fashions of time and race; and just as a wise man—still more a wise woman—will show wisdom by not pedantically resisting fashions of dress, or even speech—so it is a poor singularity which, in an age unembarrassed in its tears, essays heroic restraint. The dry eyes of a Jane Austen do not make me like her much the better; and I hardly begin to understand Achilles until he tosses on his bed and cries like a child. This was something, truly, that Plato did *not* understand; but then Plato *was*—or a part of him was—a sentimentalist. It should be added that in both the Wordsworths there was, as in so many others whom the Lake Country bred, or sheltered, a deep strain of hypochondria; and when Wordsworth spoke of

Dorothy's ' nervous blubbering ' he was scolding a failing of race. It is worth remembering, further, that the Wordsworths (and Coleridge) lived a life very much directed to one another as well as away from the world. The conditions of it had an antique simplicity almost artificial in its completeness: and this bare simplicity, this narrow range of intercourse, discouraged many restraints which a larger and less elemental intercourse imposes as a kind of law of health. Moreover, these conditions broke down other barriers. To the partners of such an environment, it is open to be a good deal more honest and sensible upon a great number of subjects than souls less antique. Thus it happens that, of any two superficial observers, one will be tempted to call Dorothy sentimental, and another, equally mistaken, to think of her as a degree matter-of-fact. Like Wordsworth himself, she drives her roots deep into a soil of north-country *sense*. She has a certain Cumberland canniness or shrewdness. Wordsworth had it in a yet greater degree; and as he grew older, it tended to impair parts of his sensibility. This does not happen with Dorothy—or it is not traceable. But the paradox of both of them is the interaction of a passionate sensibility with a matter-of-fact acceptance of what is and happens for what it is worth. I know not how better to express this than to say that they are both romantics—with a *canny romanticism*.

Both of them possessed great physical hardiness or hardness. Dorothy's long walks were so long as to be thought unladylike—in an age of ' misses '. Wordsworth himself compares her to a shepherd-boy; and from one of her letters to Jane Pollard, we learn that, when those ' very amiable young men ', the Pinneys,

were at Racedown, she indulged herself with them
'riding sometimes, hunting, coursing, cleaving wood'[1]
—a sentimentalist who, at least to her prim relations,
must have appeared a veritable virago. These 'glad
animal movements' are a most real part of Dorothy;
and it is all-important to remember that both she and
Wordsworth—as Wordsworth never forgets—made their
first contact with Nature in very normal boy-and-girl
fashion. To the spirit of boy-and-girl adventure in the
open succeeds that mood of 'wild ecstasy' in which rock
and cataract come to haunt the mind 'like a passion';
and to that mood succeeds the mood of which we are
accustomed to think as distinctively, or exclusively,
Wordsworthian—

> that serene and blessed mood
> In which the affections gently lead us on. . . :

Dorothy's work and worth in life are summed in what
she meant to her brother and to Coleridge. It is for that
that we still read her prolix and often trivial diaries; and,
indeed, it was for that that she wrote them, and wrote
them as they are written. I use the hard words 'prolix
and trivial' without any connotation of blame. They
are applicable to a great part of Dorothy's journals in
exactly the same fashion as they are applicable to a great
part of Wordsworth's poetry; and for exactly the same
reason—Wordsworth. Wordsworth and Dorothy, as I
have said, used one and the same note-book; and whatever we find in the diaries was put there for Wordsworth
to see. Where the diaries record some experience which
Dorothy and her brother had shared, it is impossible but

---

[1] Harper, i. 293.

that Dorothy's record should preserve her brother's perceptions and comment; and even when she describes, for her brother, what she alone had seen, we have always the sense that she has tried to see object or incident as *he* would have seen it. In saying that I neither question her absolute truthfulness of eye, nor disparage her sensibility —few women have had either more truthful senses or a more receptive heart. But these two persons with one soul are, in the diaries, as I think, so intermixed that it would have perplexed either to have to cry *meum* and *tuum*. The famous sonnet on Westminster Bridge is given already in prose in Dorothy's journal.[1] The village funeral which Dorothy saw, in Wordsworth's absence, on the 3rd September, 1800, appears in the journal under that date, only to reappear in the second book of the *Excursion*; and there are numerous other examples of this common property in emotional experiences. There are passages of Dorothy's journal of which the reader is moved to feel that they had been better done in verse; and there are passages of Wordsworth's poems in which he is sensible that prose had been the fitter medium. It is idle to ask, how many of the best things in the diaries are due to Wordsworth; but it is at least worth observing in this connexion (what I have indeed noted elsewhere) that Wordsworth's insistence on the value, for poetry, of accurate observation sometimes led both him and Dorothy into being tedious and trivial; and that the journals may very well have induced in Wordsworth the habit, in which we so often catch him out, of observing his own observation, and losing, in doing so, the gleam and glow of a first perception.

It remains true that much that is recorded in the

[1] Cited by Mr. Nichol Smith, *Wordsworth, Prose and Poetry*, p. 208.

diaries—particularly in the earlier diaries—has been observed with a poet's eye.

' The sound of the sea distinctly heard on the tops of the hills, which we could never hear in summer. We attribute this partly to the bareness of the trees, but chiefly to the absence of the singing of birds, the hum of insects, that noiseless noise which lives in the summer air.' *There* if any one feels inclined to cry ' Wordsworth ' (for nothing could be more Wordsworthian), at least let him remember that it was of Dorothy that Wordsworth said ' She gave me eyes, she gave me ears '. Lesser effects are almost equally fine—I choose almost at random : ' The road to the village of Holford glittered like another stream' ; ' The still trees only gently bowed their heads, as if listening to the wind ' ; ' I was much amused with the busyness of a pair of stonechats ; their restless voices as they skimmed along the water, following each other, their shadows under them, and then returning back to the stones on the shore, chirping with the same unwearied voice . . . Grasmere very solemn in the last glimpse of twilight. It calls home the heart to quietness ' ; ' The waves round about the little Island seemed like a dance of Spirits that rose out of the water' ; ' Our favourite birch-tree. It was yielding to the gusty wind with all its tender twigs. The sun shone upon it, and it glanced in the wind like a flying sunshiny shower. It was a tree in shape, with stem and branches, but it was like a Spirit of water '.

The method of observation which these chance-assorted quotations illustrate is revealed to us by a casual expression in the journals themselves. Writing on the 30th April, 1802, ' I did not sleep ' Dorothy says, ' but lay with half-shut eyes looking at the prospect as on a vision almost, I was so resigned to it'. That the observation of the poet is necessarily vision, we need not pause to re-affirm; but the phrase 'resigned to it' is arresting. This 'resignation' is what Wordsworth, in one of the poems of *Lyrical Ballads*, calls the mind's 'wise passiveness'; and in this passivity of the senses all genuine poetic perception (he believed) begins. The verses have already been cited,[1] and their implications noted.

Of humour, there are, as we might expect, few touches. The description of the old lady at Rydal who 'was an affecting picture of patient disappointment suffering under no particular affliction' might pass, if we met it in Miss Austen, for a stroke of gentle satire. But Dorothy is just saying, I think, what she found, in the first words that come, with no malice in the rear-guard of them. March 11th, 1798, offers, indeed, an odd sally of humour: 'Met the blacksmith. Pleasant to see the labourer on Sunday jump with the friskiness of a cow upon a sunny day.' And yet, I hardly know. I can conceive Wordsworth seizing that and transferring it, I will not say to the great Ode, to the stanza where—a little absurdly—the 'young lambs bound As to the tabor's sound', but at least to such a piece as 'Stray Pleasures'—and never a smile or pucker lighten that Covenanting countenance.

Literary history affords only one example of a friendship between brother and sister more affecting than that between Wordsworth and Dorothy; I mean of course the friendship of Charles and Mary Lamb. There is something like an inversion of the relationship there; the ministering office falls to the man.[2] But where, I

---
[1] p. 110.
[2] In his old age the ministering office fell, of course, to Words-

sometimes wonder, where would Lamb have been, through the terrible crises hourly apprehended of Mary's sickness, without that all-supporting gift of humour, that brave kindly grace ? We can only guess from those two unforgettable letters which he wrote to Coleridge, in September and October 1796[1]—letters which, just because they are not literature, are painful to read, to a degree almost insupportable.

It has been remarked, and it is, indeed, notable, that religious reflection has no place at all in Dorothy's diaries. The dates of them add to the significance of this. The published portions take in the years 1798, 1800, 1802 ; they cover, that is, a period in Wordsworth's life when he had not yet made that return upon orthodoxy which coincides so remarkably, in time, with the decline of his poetical powers. Did Dorothy share in the early adventure of his free-thinking ? Mrs. Wordsworth certainly did not. Even as late as 1824 the ' trembling fear ' of Wordsworth's faith gave pain to her more settled orthodoxy, his half-doubts ' offended ' her ' humbleness ' (see the poem ' O dearer far than light and life are dear '). But the mind of Dorothy was more daring ; she was more like Wordsworth himself. Wordsworth, be it remembered, in his early period questioned not only the accepted religion, but conventional morality. There can be little doubt that, in his Godwinian period, he shared Godwin's opinions as to the sanctity of the marriage tie. Indeed, the more I reflect upon the much discussed Annette episode, the more I seem to find the most probable explanation of it in a stubborn intellectual

---

worth, and to his wife and daughter. But the call upon Lamb's unaided youth is something different.

[1] Lucas, Letters 8 and 9.

daring. The secret of this episode Dorothy seems to have shared from the beginning; and it would seem neither to have dismayed nor to have depressed her masculine understanding. She had all the facts, of which we have but furtive echoes; and here once again, just as in connexion with the more baffling errancies of Coleridge, I would rather trust her judgement than my own—or Bishop Wordsworth's.

Dorothy seems to have maintained with Annette a fairly regular correspondence. It is only recently that we have come to know anything—we have to thank M. Legouis for it—of Annette's qualities and disposition. To be perfectly plain, she would seem to have been a girl of more temperament than sense, and of little or no education. M. Legouis is not sure that she had so much as discovered that Wordsworth wrote poetry—still less that he was a poet. If she knew it, I doubt whether it very much interested her. M. Legouis has printed a long letter which she wrote to Dorothy; and it can hardly have escaped Dorothy's quick intuition that it was, not to speak too harshly, a rather trivial and vulgar composition. To her at least it was patent that William had made a mistake—that, moral questions quite apart, Annette was an inconceivable companion for him. None the less, it was William's mistake; and as such, Dorothy shouldered it bravely. She wrote regularly to Annette; she stood with William against the affronted respectability of his relations; and twice she travelled with him to France to meet, and be with, Annette. Annette, be it added in fairness, was a girl of a fine courage, a *Chouane* who held her life cheap in comparison with causes that captivate imagination. Here at least was something which could appeal to Dorothy's generous soul.

Much of Dorothy's journals and letters still lies in manuscript. I am not over-curious to see it; and rather hope, indeed, that I never shall. I think that we know enough; and that there is not room in the world for a biography of Dorothy. At no time had she any thoughts that were not Wordsworth's; and her every action tended to him. I do not forget Coleridge; but to Dorothy, I fancy, the two men were one piece of greatness; and what distinctions the woman in her made, the saint, or poetess, in her forthwith annulled. It is profitless to claim for her, what she would never have dreamed of claiming for herself, an independent place in literature. She was more than content to be a footnote to Wordsworth, or a bold, but tearful, *plaudite* to the tragi-comedy of Coleridge. She has a great deal more than what she was more than content with. She has a permanent place in the affections of all who have felt the power of these two great poets—or of poetry. It is not a little thing to know greatness; to know it better than it knows itself; to know it long before the world does; to maintain in it, through ridicule and obloquy, and amidst its frailties, unshaken confidence; to have it with one daily and domestically, with all the jars of its irritability, its alternations of fever and languor, and yet to see it always in glorifying distance, the roughnesses not reckoned in the transcending reach and mass. All that is not little, and, we know, each one of us, not easy. With the women of the Wordsworth family self-effacing study made it easy. That seems to be true of all of them. It is difficult to read anything about any of them without a catch in the heart. Dorothy is best known, and comes nearest to us; not merely by accident, but she owes it to temperament and talent. If her life of constant service looks, now, easy and natural, that is because there is a genius of service ; which she had. But it came to her not without pains and tears. ' Nervous blubbering,' says Wordsworth roughly. ' It is not so ' she says, in her plain uncensuring way. I have sometimes thought that one's fitness to be a student of Wordsworth might be measured by one's power to comment upon him in Dorothy's truthful uncomplaining fashion.

PRINTED IN GREAT BRITAIN
AT THE UNIVERSITY PRESS, OXFORD
BY VIVIAN RIDLER
PRINTER TO THE UNIVERSITY